The S   the Stories

Patricia St. John

Irene Howat

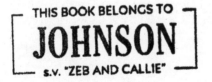

CF4•K

Written for:
Margaret Ann, Tom, Susan and their families

Copyright © 2008 Christian Focus Publications
ISBN 978-1-84550-328-4

Christian Focus Publications
Geanies House, Fearn, Tain, Ross-shire, IV20 1TW,
Scotland, United Kingdom
www.christianfocus.com
email: info@christianfocus.com

Thinking Further Topics; Life Summary and Timeline
Copyright © 2008 Christian Focus Publications

Cover design by Daniel van Stratten
Cover illustration by Neil Reed

Printed and bound in Denmark
by Nørhaven Paperback A/S

Contents

Fun and Games

'This hill seems to get steeper every day!' Mum laughed. 'Or perhaps it's just that you're growing too big to be pushed around in a pram, Oliver.'

Two-year-old Oliver certainly looked as though he could manage up the hill on his own sturdy legs, but in 1923 little children were pushed around in high prams much longer than they are today.

'Let me help,' said Patricia, who was all of four and a half.

Lending all of her strength to the job, the girl helped her mother push the giggling Oliver right to the top of the hill.

'Let's run!' she laughed, when they were over the top.

'Let's not bother,' Mum said firmly. 'We don't want Oliver in a crumpled heap at the bottom of the hill.'

Patricia looked up at her mother and smiled.

'Tell me that story, please,' she said. 'It's my most favourite story of all.'

Mrs St. John remembered back to 1919 and was not sure if it was one of her favourite stories, even though it did have a happy ending.

'Well,' she said, 'it all began far away on the other side of the world.'

Patricia held on to the handle of Oliver's pram and listened to what her mother was saying. Although she had heard the story over and over again, sometimes when her mother told it she added little bits that the girl didn't already know. It was something of a game for Patricia to find new facts each time it was told.

'Your dad and I were missionaries in Brazil in South America. And that's where your big brother and sister were born.'

'I'm glad I wasn't born there,' Patricia laughed. 'Hazel and Farnham said that there were so many black beetles in the house that the legs of their beds had to sit inside tins of kerosene to keep the beetles from running all over their faces!'

'Did they indeed!' laughed her mother. 'They must have heard that from Dad. But they've got it wrong, because that was in our first little home in Buenos Aires, and we lived there before either of them were born!'

Patricia looked rather sad about that for it was such a good story.

'Do you want me to go on?' asked Mum.

Suddenly remembering what she had asked her mother to tell her, the girl smiled and said that she did.

'Dad travelled long distances in his work, often riding on horseback over high mountain passes to reach little villages where people didn't know about the Lord.

Eventually Dad and another missionary decided that we should move to Brazil and set up a Bible School in Carangola. That was quite a move, I can tell you,' Mum recalled. 'Hazel was just the same age as Oliver is now and Farnham was only seven weeks old.'

Patricia grinned. 'Was that when you lived in the House of a Thousand Fleas' she asked, 'or have Hazel and Farnham got that wrong too?'

'No, that's right enough,' her mother laughed. 'And what a good time we had there for a while. But Farnham became ill and he seemed not to be getting better at all, whatever I did for him. He had a very nasty disease called dysentery and the poor little lamb had very sore ears too. I'm afraid your brother wasn't a happy little boy at all. He just seemed to get thinner and paler as the days went past. By then the Bible School was open and Dad had been asked to go to even more remote places to start more Bible Schools.'

Patricia's mind was in far-away Brazil and her young heart wished that she had been born there ... fleas and all!

'Let's sit down for a minute,' suggested Mrs St. John. 'There's a bench just here and the sun is shining right on it.'

They sat down and let Oliver out of the pram to toddle on the grass for a while.

'What happened then?' Patricia asked, although she knew the whole story very well indeed.

'Dad and I prayed about what we should do and felt that the Lord was showing us that we should return home to England for a time and that Dad should then go back to South America and I should live here with you children.'

'But I wasn't born then,' laughed the girl.

'I'm just coming to that,' her mother assured her.

'We came home by boat. It was so stormy. In fact, as we went through the Bay of Biscay there was such a storm blowing that I was sure you would be born in the middle of it!'

'That would have been exciting!' Patricia said.

Her mother ignored her!

'Eventually we reached Southampton on the south coast of England, and booked into a little place for the night before heading back home to Malvern, where we thought you were to be born. You were due about four weeks later.'

'We were so pleased to be back on dry land,' Mum remembered, 'that Dad decided we should all go for a walk to enjoy it. So he borrowed a big pram and put Farnham safely into it. Hazel, who was tired after the long journey, was put on top and we set out to investigate St Leonards, near Southampton, where we were staying. Dad was so proud to be pushing his children along the road, something he had never done before because the tracks around Carangola were not suitable for prams. But I'm afraid that he was not a very good pram driver!'

Patricia held her breath. She knew exactly what was coming.

'When we reached the top of a hill he and the pram got in a muddle and it went racing down the hill with your dad desperately hanging on with one hand. The inevitable happened. The pram eventually toppled and Hazel and Farnham were thrown to the ground. Thankfully, because it was February, they were warmly wrapped up and their clothes stopped them from being hurt, although you wouldn't have known that from their screams!'

'I suppose they were screaming because they got such a fright,' suggested the girl.

'And they weren't the only ones who got a fright!' Mum laughed. 'For, as you know, I got such a fright that you, Patricia Mary St. John, were born a few hours later!'

'Do you know what I think is funniest about that story?' the child asked.

'No,' admitted Mum.

'I think it's funny that you went into the hotel with two children and when you went away you had three!'

Mrs St. John laughed. 'Well,' she said, 'I can't remember whether the kind lady asked us to pay extra for you or not! But we did have to stay longer than just one night.'

Oliver toddled up to his sister.

'Me want in,' he said, pointing to his pram.

'I suppose it's time to be going,' said Mum, lifting the little lad into the pram and clipping his straps safely to each side.

Patricia gave Oliver his fluffy pom-pom ball. 'Mum and I will both hold on to your pram at the top of the hill so that it doesn't run away, because we don't want another new baby tonight.'

Mrs St. John looked very surprised at the thought.

'No,' she laughed out loud. 'We certainly do not!'

Hazel, Farnham, Patricia and Oliver had a happy childhood at Malvern in England, where they lived with their mother, grandmother and great-grandmother. Their home, a three-storey house called Holmesdale, often had other children visiting too.

'Why don't you have a daddy?' a visitor asked Patricia one day.

'I do have a daddy,' she said. 'It's just that he doesn't live with us all the time.'

The child was puzzled. 'Why not?' she asked.

Hazel, who had overheard the conversation, decided to come to her little sister's rescue.

'Our dad's a missionary,' she explained. 'That means he goes to people who don't know about the Lord Jesus Christ and tells them about the Saviour.'

'But everybody knows about Jesus,' the child said.

'Everybody here does,' Hazel agreed. 'That's why Dad's in South America. Many people there don't know about him at all.'

'Does he come home at weekends?' she was asked.

Hazel tried not to laugh at her young interrogator.

'Come and let me show you where South America is,' she said, leading the child to a globe of the world.

'Look, here's England, and we're here,' she said, using a pencil to point out Malvern. 'Now,' she went on, turning the globe round slowly, 'that's Brazil.'

'It's on the other side of the world!' exclaimed the child.

Hazel nodded. 'That's why Dad doesn't come home at weekends. But he does come home as often as he can. And it's very exciting when he comes because he has so many stories to tell us.'

'Have you ever been to visit your dad in Brazil?'

Laughing, Hazel explained that she'd been born there.

'You can't have been,' said the child. 'You don't have black skin!'

It took some time for Hazel to explain that the children of white parents are white wherever in the world they are born, and that Brazilian people don't have black skins anyway!

When Patricia was five years old she was sent away on a short holiday.

'There's a surprise for you when you go home,' said Great Aunt Emmie.

Patricia's eyes shone. 'What kind of surprise?'

The old lady knew how to keep secrets.

'I can't tell you any more than that the surprise is something to play with and that it's alive.'

That night, as the girl lay in bed, all sorts of pictures went through her mind.

'I wonder if it's a puppy,' she thought, imagining herself playing on the grass with a friendly little dog. 'Or it may be a kitten.' Then her imagination produced a picture of a fluffy tabby kitten rolled up in a ball in the sun. And in the morning when she awoke, Patricia's first thought was that the new lively toy was definitely a kitten. When she was taken home again, she rushed into the house asking to be shown where the kitten was.

'Kitten?' was her grandmother's puzzled response. 'You don't have a kitten, dear,' she said. 'You have a new little brother. His name's John.'

Not too long afterwards the family did get a kitten, which became a cat that produced kittens of its own. And they were born one night in Patricia's bed while she was sound asleep! The St. John children also had rabbits, but they were not popular with the next door neighbours.

'Really, Mrs St. John, I must protest about your children's rabbits,' said the taller of the two Miss Wheelers. 'They have been in our garden yet again!'

'I am sorry,' Mum said soothingly, 'I'm afraid they are very mischievous.'

The shorter Miss Wheeler, who had come with her

sister to the door, shook her head in such a way that Mum just knew she was thinking that the children were even more mischievous than their rabbits.

'Please try to control them,' said the taller Miss Wheeler. 'They've eaten some of our cabbages.'

'Of course I will,' Mum promised, wondering how to keep her promise. It seemed that whatever they did the rabbits could find their way through the railings and into the next door garden.

Farnham and Patricia, who were cross at the Misses Wheeler for upsetting their mother, decided to pay their neighbours a visit.

'Let's wait until its dark,' suggested Farnham to his young sister.

She nodded and grinned at the prospect of carrying out the plan they'd hatched when huddled up together in the cupboard at the top of the stairs.

'Ready?' asked Patricia, when her grandmother had closed the sitting-room curtains.

'Ready,' nodded Farnham.

The pair of them went into the kitchen as though they were going to do nothing more interesting than drink a glass of milk.

'What are you two up to?' asked the family cook. 'You have mischief written all over your faces.'

Farnham grinned. 'We're just going out into the back garden,' he said. 'We won't be long.'

Elsie looked at him long and hard before treating

Patricia to the same stare, but neither gave anything away.

Two minutes later Elsie knew exactly what they were up to. From the garden next door came the yowling and screeching of two tom cats … or two children pretending to be tom cats. Laughing at the noise, and at the cheek of the mischiefs, she continued washing the tea dishes. The noise grew louder and louder and louder.

'Maybe I should bring the young scamps in,' thought Elsie.

Just then, having had no response from the Misses Wheeler, Farnham and Patricia turned their attention to the Misses Heathcote, who stayed on their other side. Once again the eerie wails of tom cats were heard. Elsie decided that enough was enough. But just as she opened the back door she heard the next door's kitchen window being pulled up.

'Take that!' the Misses Heathcote's cook shouted out the window.

Correctly guessing what had happened, Elsie held the door open for two drenched children to race in, giggling fit to burst!

'She really thought we were tom cats,' Patricia said, laughing aloud as soon as the door was safely closed.

'Did you hear us?' asked Farnham.

'I think everyone in Alexandra Road heard you,' she replied. 'Now, I suggest you get these wet clothes off and put on your night things before your grandmother discovers what you've been up to. She might have something to say about it.'

By the time Grandmother next saw Farnham and Patricia they were dry and ready for bed.

'You're dear children' she said, as she wished them goodnight.

And Elsie, who was just finishing for the night, heard her, shook her head and smiled.

Great-grandmother, who was quite old and frail, spent most of her time in bed. Although she loved all the children, she and Oliver had a special friendship. One afternoon, Patricia's mother was in the sitting room totally unable to speak. She was laughing so much.

'What's funny?' asked Patricia.

Mum couldn't answer a word!

Greatly puzzled, the girl waited … and waited until her mother had recovered herself enough to talk.

'You know that Oliver loves sitting on Great-grandmother's bed talking to her,' said Mrs St. John. 'Well, half an hour ago I left them looking at a picture book together. Of course, I knew Oliver would change the subject to trains as soon as I closed the door. He has trains on his brain, that young man.'

Patricia watched her mother's face. She loved a good story, and any story her mother told was told well.

'A few minutes ago I went back and you'll never guess what I discovered.'

'What?' begged the girl. 'What were they doing?'

'Oliver had pulled three bedroom chairs out into the middle of the room and set them one behind the other to make his very own train. He was sitting on the first one pretending to drive the engine and Great-grandmother was sitting on the middle one, with her long nightgown draped right down to the floor. She was bouncing gently up and down saying, "Puff puff, puff puff, puff puff!"'

Patricia thought she had never heard anything funnier and couldn't wait to tell Hazel and Farnham.

Goodbye and Bonjour!

When Patricia St. John was still five years old her great-grandmother died. That was a very strange time in Holmesdale.

'I feel sad and happy at the very same time,' Hazel said. And that described exactly how Patricia felt too.

'I'm sad because I'll miss Great-grandmother,' she agreed. 'I loved her very much. But I'm happy because she's in heaven with Jesus and she's not old or ill any more.'

Poor Oliver, who had lost his very best friend, just didn't know what to do with himself. He kept going to her room and sitting on her bed as though she were still there to tell him a story.

'Would you like me to tell you a story?' asked Hazel, who was a kind-hearted child. 'It won't be as good as Great-grandmother's stories, but it's about a little boy just like you.'

Oliver looked at her hopefully. And when his older sister told him the story of a little boy who put three chairs in a row in order to play trains with his great-grandmother, he smiled for the first time since the old lady died.

* * *

The following morning the sun woke Patricia early.

'What day is it?' she wondered.

As she didn't go to school, she had to think for a minute before she remembered it was Sunday. Then she grinned.

'This is my favourite day of the week,' she told Polly, her doll, who was cuddled up in bed with her. 'And you can join in this afternoon, if you like.'

Polly lay silent and Patricia took that for a yes.

But morning comes before afternoon every day, and Sunday morning in Holmesdale meant putting on stiff uncomfortable clothes.

'Stand still, please,' said Grandmother, as she pulled Patricia's liberty bodice over her head.

'Why does it have rubber buttons?' the girl asked, 'rather than ordinary ones?'

'I don't know,' admitted her grandmother, 'but that's what all liberty bodices have. I suppose it stops them slipping out of the buttonholes in your pantaloons.'

Thinking of all the times she had had to rush to the toilet and struggle to undo these silly rubber buttons, Patricia wished that they weren't there at all!

'Now, put on your petticoat and brush your hair a hundred times before you pull on your frock.'

Patricia brushed her hair a hundred times each morning and evening. But that was just one of the many things she had to do before she was fit to be seen in public. It was like a military operation getting children ready for church in the 1920s as they had so many clothes to wear, some of them starched stiff, and a number of them with buttons to be done, bows to be tied and hooks to be hooked as well.

'Have you all got your Bibles?' Mum asked.

Hazel, Farnham, Patricia and Oliver held up their Bibles. Baby John held up his hand, but just to wave goodbye as he was staying at home with his grandmother.

'I wonder if the Stayputs will be in church today?' Patricia asked herself as they headed out the door. 'I imagine they all brush their hair a million times each morning!'

The Stayputs were there! They were four sisters who went to the same church as the St. Johns when they visited family in Malvern, and they were so well-behaved! Of course, The Stayputs wasn't their real name; it was probably Farnham who thought it up.

'I bet they don't move the whole of the service,' whispered Hazel to Farnham.

'Christians shouldn't bet,' teased her brother. 'The Stayputs can't move anyway,' he added. 'They have brush handles inside their coats so that they can't move.'

Mrs St. John looked at her oldest daughter and smiled. Somehow Mum's smile helped Hazel to behave much more than if she'd been cross with her. It made all the children want to be good.

* * *

Sunday services seemed very, very long. The little Brethren church had no organ or piano, no flowers and no coloured glass windows to look at. The walls were the colour of mud, the hard benches the children sat on creaked each time they moved, and they moved quite often. But although it was very simple and plain, something of what they heard usually pushed its way into the children's brains. It had to, for Grandmother would question them about the service as soon as they went in the door of Holmesdale. Patricia smiled at the memory of some of their answers to Grandmother's question, 'What happened at the service today?'

'A cat came into the hall this morning,' she was told once. 'And an old man had to chase it out.'

'Oliver giggled because he thought the preacher read from Paul's letter to the Galoshes, rather than his letter to the Colossians,' was another happening faithfully carried home and reported.

'Good morning, children,' said the man at the church door as they left. 'You could learn how to sit without making the benches squeak if you studied our little visitors,' he whispered to Oliver loudly enough for all to hear.

Patricia thought of The Stayputs and wanted to poke them!

Lunch over, the St. John children prepared themselves for a splendid afternoon.

'Whose turn is it to get the Sunday box out?' asked Oliver.

It was Farnham's turn. He made a great show of dragging it into the middle of the floor where everyone could get around it. Mum brought her special Sunday bag and all the children wondered what was inside it this week. But first the children had their very own Sunday Special. Although Patricia did not attend school she could read and this was the tastiest reading possible.

'Spread out the letters,' Mum told Oliver, who couldn't do it quickly enough.

He opened the tin and spread out all the little biscuits his mother had made. Each one was in the shape of a letter of the alphabet! Although he was just learning his letters, Oliver knew enough to put all the As together, all the Bs together, all the Cs together, right to the end of the alphabet. And even Xs and Zs were included, because they were sometimes needed for this Sunday game.

'You go first, Patricia,' said Mum.

The girl opened her Bible, found a short verse and then made the verse out of the biscuit letters.

'Now read it to me and tell me where it comes in the Bible,' Grandmother said.

'They're words Jesus said,' Patricia told the family. 'It says, "I am the good shepherd," and it's from John chapter ten and verse eleven.'

'May I have a turn?' asked Farnham, who sometimes

23

felt he was too old for the game. 'I know a verse that will use a Z and an X.'

Choosing the letters carefully, and not eating any of them, he wrote: 'Zacchaeus, he was a chief tax collector and was wealthy,' he read, 'and that's in Luke nineteen verse two.'

The rules of the game were that the letters had to be made into verses and learned by the children before the letter-shaped biscuits could be eaten. It was amazing how quickly even the littlest ones could learn a verse when there was a tasty biscuit to eat as a reward! By the time the biscuits were finished John was sleeping, and even Oliver had nodded off in front of the fire. Hazel, Farnham and Patricia were not sorry as that gave them their mother all to themselves for the rest of the afternoon.

'Would you like a story first, or do you want to do your missionary books before that?'

All three decided on a story.

'Far away in China,' Mum began, 'there was a family who knew nothing about the Lord Jesus Christ. They had never even heard his name. One day a little servant girl went to live and work in their home. She lived in a little cupboard off their kitchen. It was dark there but warm because the cooking was done over an open fire. So even in winter, when it's very cold in China, the little girl stayed cosy. She had been brought up in a Christian home and loved the Lord Jesus with all her heart.'

'What was her name?' Hazel asked.

'I don't know the answer to that,' admitted Mum. 'As I said, it was very cold in the winter in China. One of the servant girl's jobs was to gather wood for the kitchen fire. This meant walking a long way in all kinds of weather. One winter it was so very cold that all the local wood was used up and she had to go really far away to collect fuel for the fire. Her padded jacket was wet in the rain and she didn't have any clothes to change into. I'm afraid her little body became chilled and even the kitchen fire couldn't heat her through.'

Farnham nudged his sisters, who were sitting on either side of him, and then he nodded towards his mother. Her mind was far away in the China of long ago and tears flowed down her face as she thought about the shivering little servant.

'Day after day she walked for miles, and night after night the little girl arrived home damp and chilled to the bone,' Mrs St. John went on. 'Every night, before she went to sleep, she clasped her hands together in prayer and asked the Lord to bless her and her mother and father, brothers and sisters. One morning the cook found the dear little child lying dead in her bed.'

'That's a really sad story,' Hazel said. 'Is that the end of it?'

'Not quite,' Mum said. 'Some time later a poor woman arrived at the house and asked to speak to the cook. It was the little girl's mother who had been sent a message saying that her daughter had died in her sleep.

When she was taken to the kitchen she asked the cook how the girl had been lying when she was found. The cook thought that was a very strange question to ask, and then he remembered that when he found the child she had been lying with her hands clasped in front of her. The poor woman's sad face broke into a beautiful smile. "Why are you smiling?" asked the cook. The woman explained to him that her daughter had been speaking to the Lord Jesus before she died and that now she was alive in heaven with the Lord whom she loved. The wonderful end of the story is that the cook was so impressed by what the little girl's mother told him that he asked her about the Lord Jesus and eventually trusted in the Saviour himself!'

Patricia looked at her mother and saw tears running down her face. She couldn't work out whether they were tears of sadness at the little girl dying, or tears of joy that the cook had become a Christian. Then she thought back just a few months to when her great-grandmother died and remembered that sometimes you can't separate sadness and joy from each other.

'Is it time for our missionary books?' Farnham asked, because the previous Sunday he had been fascinated by what he'd discovered about the faraway land of Paraguay.

His mother smiled. 'Yes, it is,' she said, and Hazel, Farnham and Patricia opened the Sunday box and took out their missionary books.

'What are we doing today?' Hazel asked.

'I don't think we quite finished last Sunday,' her mother remembered. 'We'd read the letter from the missionaries working in Paraguay, but I didn't show you the pictures they sent. I wonder how much you remember about Paraguay.'

The children smiled. They knew Mum was testing them, but her tests always felt like a game and they enjoyed them.

'Do you remember what countries surround Paraguay?' she asked.

'Brazil, Bolivia and Argentina,' answered Farnham.

'Well done! Now for a more difficult question. Can you tell me what two languages the people speak?'

'They speak Spanish,' Patricia said confidently.

'And Guarani,' added Farnham.

'I knew the answers too, but they always seem to answer first!' Hazel complained.

Her mother laughed. 'Now you know what I feel like when Grandmother asks me a question and you three all answer her before I do!'

All the children laughed! That happened quite often. Just then their mother reached into her Sunday bag - now they were going to find out what was inside!

'Last week I read you a letter from missionaries working in Paraguay,' mother reminded them. 'But what I didn't show you was a set of drawings they enclosed with the letter.'

The children looked through the drawings. Some of them were of children in an outdoor Sunday School, one was of the Bible School, and several were of the missionary's family.

'These are lovely,' Hazel said softly. 'But aren't they too good to paste into our scrap books?'

'I think they should go in,' suggested Mum, 'because I hope you will keep these scrapbooks until you are grown up to help you remember about the missionaries we've heard from over the years.'

What Mrs St. John didn't know, but perhaps hoped would happen, was that Patricia would still treasure her missionary scrap book when she was a very old lady.

It was after a very happy Sunday, and yet another story about a little Christian girl who died and went home to heaven, that Patricia prayed a special prayer. Before the Chinese girl died she had copied a verse from the Bible. Patricia copied the very same verse. It said, 'But now, this is what the Lord says … I have redeemed you; I have called you by name; you are mine' (Isaiah 43:1).

'My name is Patricia,' she said to the Lord before going to bed that night. 'And if you are really calling me, I want to come and be yours.'

Years later, Patricia St. John remembered that the next morning, when she went into the garden and looked at the tall hollyhock flowers, she thought that she had never before seen anything quite so beautiful.

* * *

When Patricia was seven years old, her mother and father made a very interesting decision. Mr St. John would continue his work in South America and his wife and children would move to Switzerland for a year.

'Switzerland!' the children said together, when they were told the news.

Actually John didn't understand what he was saying, but he did like to copy his older brothers and sisters.

'What will we do there?' Hazel asked, already excited at the thought.

'Just what you do here,' answered her mother. 'You'll go to school, do your homework, help in the house, read your books and play outside in the warm Swiss summer and in the crisp winter snows.'

'But I don't go to school here,' Patricia reminded her mother. 'You teach me.'

'Your father and I think that it would be good for you to start school in Switzerland. That way you'll learn French more quickly than if you stayed at home with me and the little ones.'

Patricia felt a surge of excitement rush through her. School! Then fear took its place. French! 'But I don't know any French!' she wailed. 'I'll not understand anything people say to me!'

Mrs St. John lifted her daughter on to her knee. 'You'll learn French very quickly when it's being spoken all around you,' she told Patricia. 'And before we go we'll teach you one French word each day.'

The child's eyes shone.

'Today's word is "bonjour" and it means "good day" or "hello",' Mum told her.

'Bonjour!' Patricia repeated happily. 'Bonjour! Bonjour! Bonjour!'

Then she disappeared through to the kitchen to tell everyone that she could speak French!

Packing for such a large family for a year was quite a job. But among the first things in the 'must go' pile was the Sunday box. It was quite out of the question that they should go without their missionary scrapbooks, the letters they had received from so many parts of the world, and the lovely sketches from Paraguay.

'Do I really need to take my liberty bodices?' Patricia asked, when clothes were being discussed. 'It'll be warmer in Switzerland than in England.'

'Yes, you do,' her grandmother said firmly. 'It may be warm in summer where we're going, but it will be very cold in winter. In fact, you may have to wear two liberty bodices to keep yourself warm.'

Patricia thought about that, and about all the little rubber buttons her fingers would struggle with should she need to go to the toilet quickly. She decided that however cold Switzerland was in the middle of winter, one liberty bodice would be quite enough for her!

Growing Years

'How does Mum know so much about Switzerland?' Patricia asked her grandmother, as the family travelled through France.

There was no point in asking her mother as she had a full-time job trying to keep Oliver out of mischief.

'When your mother was a little girl we had a Swiss nanny. Her name was Elise, and she talked so much about her homeland that we all felt as though we'd been brought up there ourselves! You'll meet Elise very soon. She'll be waiting to welcome us at the chalet.' And so she was.

'You see children,' Elise said, hugging Mrs St. John tightly, 'Switzerland is very, very beautiful.'

Patricia and her brothers and sister were almost unable to take in that this lovely place was to be their home for a year. That night as Patricia lay in bed the seven-year-old tried to picture the view from her window without getting up and looking out.

'There's a steep slope in front of the chalet,' she thought. 'And it goes right down to the river at the bottom of the valley. Across the valley the foot of the mountains are covered with trees in bright autumn colours and further up they are dark green with pines.

Behind them are more mountains and then even more mountains. At sunset the tops of the faraway mountains turned pink and Elise said that was because they are covered in the first winter snow.'

Although Patricia was just seven she was a noticing sort of girl. While her younger brothers spent their waking hours racing in every direction, she liked to look at things. First she would look at the thing as a whole, like a whole mountain. Then she would look at it bit by bit, noticing the autumn colours on the trees at the bottom of the mountain and the dark pine trees above them. After that she would look even more closely at the little things she could see and hear. Just before she fell asleep, Patricia remembered the sounds she had heard as she looked across the valley, the sounds of birds singing and of cowbells donging as the animals moved. She remembered the smells too, the scent of damp grass and the clean smell of pine trees. All of her life Patricia was a noticing person. That was God's special gift to her, and he had a very special use for it later in her life.

It was while the family was living in the chalet in the Montreux Oberland that Patricia went to school for the first time. 'Quel est ton nom?' she was asked by a boy in her class. She didn't understand a word he was saying, but she guessed what the question might be and told the boy her name. 'Es-tu en vacances, ou es-tu venu pour rester?' was his next question and she had no clue what the answer was to that one. She smiled and hoped she seemed friendly. But the St. John children didn't have a totally pleasant welcome.

'What's happened to you?' Granny asked one day, when Patricia arrived home dirty and bruised.

'I was pushed into a gully,' she explained. 'Then they threw stones at me.'

'Who did that?' Granny demanded.

But of course Patricia didn't know the names of any of the children who had bullied her.

Although Oliver was younger and smaller, he had quite a different way of coping. Having had a argument with a boy called Ami, he came in to tell his mother what happened.

'Mummy,' said the five-year-old, 'I think you'd better come and look at Ami. I've just killed him.'

Ami survived whatever it was Oliver did to him and things improved from then on!

The Christmas the St. Johns spent in Switzerland was one to remember. Patricia wrote to tell her father about it.

'After all the families had milked their cows they went down to the village church on their big sleighs.'

Here she drew a picture of the kind of sleighs they used – great big ones with plenty of room for the whole family.

'Most of the sleighs had cowbells on them that donged as they moved. The church was beautiful. There was a huge pine tree that made everything smell like outside because it had just been cut down that day. The church was lit with candles and they twinkled like stars. All the children sang, and I knew the words of the carol in French! We sang *Douce nuit, sainte nuit.* After the sermon the children went to the front and we were each given an orange and a gingerbread bear with white eyes and paws painted on with icing sugar! Mine is beautiful. I hope you are having a good Christmas, Daddy. We miss you and wish you were here. I love you and God loves you too. Patricia.'

The following September the whole family took a sad farewell of their lovely chalet and headed back to England, which seemed very dull and dreary by comparison. But life was never dull and dreary for long in the St. John household. With so many children and so much energy and imagination there was always something interesting going on.

'Did Auntie really say we could go to her school?' Hazel asked excitedly. 'Both of us, both Patricia and me?'

Mum smiled. 'Yes she did, though I think it will take most of her salary to pay for you both to go there.'

Mrs St. John's sister taught in a little private school near where the family lived in Malvern.

Patricia was excited beyond words. 'I'm going to school!' she sang, as she danced round the dining room table. 'And the lessons will be in English!'

* * *

While most lessons were held inside the school, some were not.

'The River Severn has burst its banks,' Matron announced one day. 'May I take the girls swimming?'

Smiling, the headmistress gave permission.

The girls were lined up in front of the school before they set off on their swimming adventure, and it was an adventure. First they had to cross the fields, jumping over cowpats as they went. Then they changed into their swimming costumes in a barn before reaching the vast floodwater of the River Severn. They were actually quite a distance away from the river's usual course, but when it burst it's banks it spread out quite deeply over several fields on either side, so deeply that the girls were able to dive off a five-bar gate into the water!

Patricia's aunt became deaf when she was in her early twenties, but she was a very determined lady and she eventually became headmistress of the school.

'I don't know how she does it,' said Hazel, as they went home from school one day. 'But Aunt seems to sense mischief and then she only needs to raise one eyebrow and everyone settles down and behaves, even you,' she concluded, winking at her little sister.

That was a fair enough comment as Patricia could be rather a scamp! 'I love when she takes the Scripture class,' she said. 'I learn things that I've never even heard from Dad and Mum.'

'I know what you mean,' agreed Hazel.

* * *

While Patricia loved school and enjoyed her lessons, she was not very keen on sports.

'I think you might be chosen for the hockey team,' her friend moaned, when the list was being made up. 'I wish I was.'

'I wish you were too,' the girl agreed, meaning every word of it.

'Patricia,' said the gym mistress a day or two later. 'I've put you in the school hockey team. Well done!'

'Oh thank you!' said Patricia. 'That's great!'

But on the way home she admitted that it wasn't great at all. Why waste Saturday afternoons hitting a poor defenceless hockey ball around when you could be enjoying yourself? And when she arrived home from school the first person who spoke to her only heard a bad-tempered grump in reply.

Later that day Patricia went for a walk. She just wanted to get away from everyone, for she knew that if any member of the family crossed her she would fly off in a rage.

'What's happening to me?' she asked herself as she walked. 'I love the family and I want to be kind and thoughtful, but when things upset me I get in such a temper.' The teenager thought back over the years. 'I suppose I've always sulked from time to time,' she admitted, 'and everyone loses their temper sometimes.' Patricia froze for a second. 'No they don't,' she admitted. Suddenly she realised that she had been stomping along the road rather than walking as she tried to find excuses for her bad moods.

Just then she noticed that she had reached the fallen tree branch. It was a place in the wood where she always sat down for a moment or two, so she did just that. By the time she started walking again she felt a little calmer. Part of the trouble was that Patricia was struggling with a guilty conscience. Having been brought up in a Christian home, it would never have occurred to her to argue about going to church or thanking God for food before every meal. But the private side of things was different. The teenager hardly ever read her Bible, and her night-time prayers were just a habit rather than something real and important to her.

Determined to be pleasant when she arrived back home, Patricia turned and headed for Holmesdale. But within a few minutes of going in the door someone annoyed her and she lost her temper completely. Feeling an utter failure, the girl rushed to her bedroom and slammed the door shut behind her. Something made her pick up her Bible; she opened it and read the words that met her eye.

'Behold, I stand at the door and knock; if any man hears my voice and opens the door, I will come in' (Revelation 3: 20).

Patricia sat down on the side of her bed. In her mind's eye she could see a little ship being blown all over the place by a storm. It had no hope of reaching the safety of the harbour. Then it was as though she heard the voice of Jesus saying, 'If you ask me in, I will take you where you want to go.'

Suddenly it was as if there was hope in her heart.

'Oh please, please come in,' she cried aloud to the Lord.

Before she went to join the rest of the family, Patricia thought back to when she was six-years-old and had told the Lord that she wanted to follow him. 'Please help me,' she prayed in her heart. And that was her prayer over and over again when, as a teenager, she felt her temper rising when things upset her. Gradually after that she found she wanted to read her Bible, and prayer began to be real rather than just part of the bedtime routine. Patricia didn't find it easy being a teenager, very few young people do, but her family was fairy relaxed and that helped a lot.

'It's amazing how your aunt's school has grown,' Mum said, when Patricia was in her final year. 'And I'm proud of you being made Head Girl.'

Patricia grinned. 'Who would ever have thought it?' she said. 'And I've really enjoyed being a boarder these last few years.'

Mrs St. John didn't say it, but she looked at her daughter and realised that being at boarding school, and having her Christian aunt as headmistress, had done her daughter a great deal of good.

'I hear that there's another house coming up for sale not far from the school,' said Mum. 'I wonder if your aunt will try to buy it.'

'She might,' Patricia agreed. 'She's bought several buildings over the last few years. And she needs them all as more and more girls board at the school.'

That's just what happened. The house, it was called Applegarth, was bought as another boarding house.

'Move to Applegarth!' said Oliver. 'But that would mean leaving Holmesdale!'

Mrs St. John nodded her head.

'I'm afraid it would,' she agreed. 'But we'll have to move from Holmesdale one day and your aunt has asked me to look after the girls boarding in Applegarth. It's a beautiful house and it would feel like home in no time at all, I'm sure.'

When the family saw Applegarth for the first time they knew that was true. It was April and the little orchard in the grounds of the house was filled with trees in blossom.

'Look!' John laughed. 'When the wind blows the cherry blossom fills the air like pink snowflakes!'

Not long after moving in, the St. Johns discovered that another family also enjoyed being in Applegarth. Hazel was living away from home by then and Patricia told her about it in a letter.

'We have ducks in the orchard and if Mum forgets to close the house doors – which she does very often

– the ducks waddle in the front door, quacking as they go, and then waddle right through the house in single file before going out the back door and into the garden again! I don't suppose the ducks do the carpets any good, but Mum loves the thought of the ducks using the house as a shortcut!'

Nurse St. John

Patricia and her two school friends stood in a huddle, shock showing on their faces.

'How could that happen?' one of them asked.

'The school sent applications off for all three of us to study medicine, but only two arrived. And the two of us have been accepted and you've not. It's awful.'

Patricia agreed that it was awful. Farnham was already studying medicine and she had hoped to do the same. Now, here she was leaving school and with nothing to do as she watched her two friends preparing to go to university. She was bitterly disappointed. But her aunt, who always saw solutions rather than problems, suggested that Patricia return to Clarendon School to help the junior teacher with children aged seven to eleven. Patricia loved it and might have chosen teaching as a career had the Second World War not been raging all around her. Nurses were needed urgently and Patricia applied for training. She started at St Thomas's Hospital in London in 1943.

'What a battle-axe the Sister is!' she thought, after her third ticking-off one morning. 'I don't even know what I did wrong that time.'

In those days nursing sisters, who were in charge of hospital wards, could be very bossy people. Patricia's night sister (nick-named the Purple Python) was one such. She insisted on a student nurse bringing dinner to her room on a tray at the stroke of midnight each night, and it had to be served beautifully. One night, at ten minutes to midnight, Patricia went into the ward kitchen just in time to see a cat running off with the Purple Python's chicken drumstick! What was she to do?

'Leave it to me,' said an older nurse. 'You go and see to the patients and I'll get it ready.'

Patricia did what she was told and then came back at a minute to midnight.

'Where did you get that?' she asked, staring at a very nicely arranged salad.

'From the bucket we put the ward's leftovers in,' the woman grinned. 'And that's all she deserves!'

Although nursing was hard, especially in wartime, Patricia loved her job even when she went through a great sadness. The only man she had ever loved and wanted to marry was killed in action. Perhaps that made her even kinder in her nursing of soldiers who had been wounded in battle.

'I admire these men so much,' she told Farnham, when they met one sunny afternoon. 'A patient died the other day and he was so brave. They all are.'

'Tell me about him,' said her brother, realising that she needed to talk.

'He was a little man from East London, a Cockney,' Patricia replied. 'When he was admitted he was desperately ill and we knew he wasn't likely to survive. If I disturbed him, he would roar at me, "I'll tell my wife on you when she comes on Sunday and I advise you to hide! My wife, she's a very big woman, and if she starts chasing you over the beds, you won't stand a chance!"'

Farnham smiled. He too was used to seeing courage in his hospital wards.

'I said he was loud,' Patricia concluded, 'but over the last few days his voice became quieter and quieter until Tuesday, when he couldn't raise the energy to talk at all. He died the following day.'

'Some of your patients do well though,' pointed out Farnham encouragingly, trying to help his sister cheer up.

'Oh yes!' smiled Patricia. 'Wait till I tell you about Reggie.'

For the next five minutes she talked about the twelve-year-old who had been admitted with meningitis. He was thought to be dying but with very careful nursing he survived, much to her delight as she spent hours trying to help the boy. That was one of the good times, but nursing had its really hard times too. At one point things were so difficult that Patricia nearly gave up. However, when she was out for a walk one day, she saw a poster that read, 'Jesus said, "Do you believe that I am able to do this?"' It was decision time. Did she believe God was able to make her into a nurse, or did she not?

'Yes,' she decided, 'I believe that he can.'

And with that in her mind and heart Patricia continued her training and passed her final exams. When she was presented with her Nightingale Badge (named after Florence Nightingale) she knew that she had God to thank for her qualifying as a nurse.

Having finished her training, Nurse St. John moved back home to Malvern to take up a job with a local doctor. But it wasn't long before her aunt persuaded her to become housemother to thirty children who were boarding at Clarendon School; they were aged seven to eleven. That was the start of a very happy two years in Patricia's life. As the parents of half of the children in her care were abroad, she was something between a housemother, a favourite aunt, and a mum to them.

'This is certainly not a boring job,' she wrote to a nursing friend. 'So far we've had a ceiling come down in a gale, heating cut off, no water because the pipes were frozen and an intruder at 10 o'clock one night. And that's before I tell you about the ups and downs, bugs and bruises, tears and laughter of the children!'

'I won't see Dad and Mum for four years,' an eight-year-old said tearfully, when she arrived at the school.

Patricia knew that what the child said was true. Today people who work abroad and have children in boarding school can usually see them during school holidays, but it was very different in the 1940s.

'I tell you what we'll do,' her housemother told her. 'Let's have a special treat tonight. Tell all the children to get into their nightclothes and dressing gowns and come down to the sitting room. We'll have some cocoa and biscuits and I'll tell them a story. While you're doing that, I'll put a match to the fire and we'll be cosy as can be. Tell everyone to bring their teddy bears.'

That became the boarding house bedtime routine.

'But what story will I tell them?' Patricia wondered, as she blew the first flickering flames of the fire into a blaze. 'I know! I'll tell them about the Good Shepherd and how Jesus cares for his lost sheep even though he has ninety-nine safe in the sheepfold. I want all the children to feel as special as that lost sheep.'

Night after night, when the children were sound asleep in bed with their teddy bears, Patricia worked on bedtime stories. She wrote pages and pages and pages!

'What are you doing?' asked Hazel, who was home for a visit.

Her sister told her.

'May I read it?'

A little hesitantly Patricia passed over a pile of sheets of paper.

'This is really good!' smiled Hazel, after over half an hour of total silence apart from the sound of pages turning. 'You should try to get it published.'

Patricia was horrified at the idea.

'Never! I wrote it for the children in the boarding house, not for publication,' she objected.

But eventually that story was published. It was called **The Tanglewoods' Secret**, and children have loved reading it ever since.

'What are you writing now?' Mum asked, some time later.

'Oh just another story for the children,' Patricia answered. 'It's based in Switzerland.'

'That must stretch your memory back!' smiled Mum. 'You were the same age as the children you look after when we lived in Switzerland.'

'True,' the young woman agreed. 'But you'd be surprised just how many tiny details I remember about our time there.'

Grandmother, who had just come into the room, nodded her head.

'I always said you were a noticing child,' she said. 'So we'd better watch out in case you notice things about us and put us in a story!'

All three laughed at the very idea.

'Will you try to publish this story?' Mum asked.

Patricia said she thought not, and it certainly seemed as if it wouldn't become a book because she left the manuscript in a public phone box and it had gone by the time she went back for it.

Mrs St. John, who had read the story, was very upset

... and very delighted when the pile of papers eventually found its way back to Patricia. That story became *Treasures of the Snow*, which is probably Patricia St. John's best-loved book. It was even made into a film!

Farnham, who by then was a doctor, felt that God wanted him to work in a missionary hospital in Tangier in North Africa. When he told his mother the news she smiled in a beautiful way. 'Sit down, the pair of you, because I have something I'd like to tell you.'

Farnham and Patricia sat down side by side by the fire.

'When you were both small children I was invited to missionary meetings in different people's homes. They were very grand homes and the ladies who went were quite rich. I felt out of place because we had so little money! People put the most amazing things in the offering plate. Some put in pearl necklaces, others put in valuable rings and brooches. These things were sold and the money went to mission work. I felt awful because I'd nothing valuable to put in. Then I realised that I did have three very valuable children, Hazel and you two. Oliver and John hadn't been born. So I prayed to the Lord and told him that I was giving the three of you to him for mission work. So I'm not surprised that he has called you to be a missionary, Farnham. It's an answer to my prayer.'

Patricia wiped her eyes. The story had really touched her heart.

That night, after she had tucked up all the children, she and Farnham settled in her sitting room for a chat.

'It must have been so hard for Mum to believe that God was answering that prayer when we were young,' she said. 'We weren't at all holy children. In fact, we were little monsters at times. When I think back to my teenage tantrums I could blush with shame.'

'I won't argue with that,' smiled Farnham. 'We all had our ups and downs. But do you remember the Hotspot Club? That must have encouraged Mum.'

Patricia smiled at the memory.

'I suppose I was about twelve at the time,' she said. 'There was the four of us and the two children who used to come and stay for the holidays because their parents were missionaries abroad.'

'That's right,' agreed Farnham. 'We decided that one day we'd all be missionaries and that we should prepare for the hard life ahead. We made up a training programme to swim a mile, sleep on the floor with no covers and walk along the high ridge of the outside toilet roof.'

Patricia shook her head. 'Shoosh!' she whispered. 'Don't tell any of the children in the boarding house about that. I don't want them all up on the roof!'

'We even cut ourselves and signed our names in blood!' remembered her brother. 'But I'm not quite sure why we thought that would be good missionary training!'

The pair of them sat quietly for a minute or two, each deep in thought.

'It's not a game now, Farnham,' said Patricia. 'It's for real. You really are going to Tangier as a missionary doctor. Mum said that she gave me to the Lord to be a missionary too. I wonder if he'll call me overseas one day.'

Her brother smiled. 'He might do. But you're already a missionary to the children in the boarding house, and to the thousands of children who've read *The Tanglewoods' Secret*.'

'I've something to show you,' said Patricia, rising from her chair and opening her desk. 'Here are two letters for you to read.'

Farnham took the letters. One was from a grandmother telling Patricia that her grandson had come to know the Lord Jesus through *The Tanglewoods' Secret*. And the other was from a little girl saying that she too had learned about Jesus in the book.

'Have you had many other letters like these?' her brother asked.

'A few more,' she admitted.

'You see what I mean, Patricia,' said Farnham. 'You're a missionary right here in England. But perhaps one day God will call you to go abroad for him.'

His sister smiled at the thought.

'Perhaps,' she said. 'Perhaps.'

Tangier!

Farnham St. John had only been in Tangier for a year when Patricia went out to join him in 1949.

'He needs a wife,' she wrote Hazel, 'but until God sends one he'll have to put up with me!'

It never occurred to her that she should apply to a missionary society before going to Tangier; she just went! Her brother lived a very hectic life and it might have kept Patricia busy just being his housekeeper, but she also worked in the hospital as a nurse.

'What does it feel like to be called by God to be a missionary?' she asked Farnham, when they had finished work one day.

He shrugged. 'It's difficult to put into words,' he said. 'I just knew in my heart that's what he wanted me to do and that Tangier is where he wanted me to be.'

Sometimes it worried Patricia that she was just there because it seemed the right thing to do at the time.

'You're nearly well enough to go home now,' she told Mohammed, who had been in hospital for many months. 'You must be looking forward to that such a lot.'

The young Moroccan man nodded his head. Of

course he was looking forward to being back in his mountain town with his family. But there was a sadness about him too, for Mohammed had listened to what the missionaries told him about the Lord Jesus and he knew that when he went home there would be nobody there to tell him any more. When the day came for him to leave hospital he was driven all the way home by Dr Farnham, and Nurse Patricia went with them for company. They left very, very early in the morning to avoid the heat of the sun, and they were some way along the road before they stopped for a picnic breakfast.

'Why do we have to go all the way to Tangier to hear about God?' asked Mohammed. 'Why can't someone come to the mountain towns and treat us when we're ill as well as telling us about the Lord?'

Farnham was delighted to hear how interested his patient was in the Bible and the two men sat for a while talking. They had left so early that Patricia hadn't had time to read her Bible, so she sat down a little distance away and began reading where she had left off the day before. She read the words, 'My sheep wandered over all the mountains and on every high hill. They were scattered over the whole earth, and no-one searched or looked for them' (Ezekiel 34: 6). Suddenly Patricia knew for sure that God was calling her to be a missionary and that he wanted her to work high on the mountains of Morocco. She didn't know when she would be able to leave Tangier and move to the mountains, but she did know that it would happen one day.

* * *

A month later, Farnham and Patricia travelled home to England for their brother John's wedding, and while they were there Farnham met the young woman he would marry. They fell in love at first sight! A few days later it was a very happy young doctor who climbed on to his motor cycle with his sister clinging on behind him to head all the way through Europe to the south of Spain in order to cross over the Mediterranean to Tangier. In fact, much of the way to Dover he sang love songs as he thought of young Dr Janet Thompson, his wife-to-be.

Patricia and her brother were too late to catch the last ferry from Dover to Calais and slept under the stars overnight. It was dark when they squirmed into their sleeping bags and they couldn't see much of where they were. The following morning Patricia woke when she heard voices nearby … but Farnham was nowhere to be seen. They had lain down to sleep at the top of a grassy bank! During the night he had rolled down the bank and was lying, fast asleep, with his legs spread out across a road. 'What's wrong?' she asked the men who were standing looking down at her sound asleep brother. 'Nothing's wrong yet,' one of them replied. 'But if you don't waken your husband and tell him to take his legs off the main London to Dover road, he'll have them cut off when the traffic starts for the day!' Laughing at the thought of Farnham being her husband,

Patricia woke him up and they were once again on their way ... still singing love songs!

* * *

Soon after they arrived back at the hospital a new nurse started work there. That, and the fact that her brother was soon to be married, meant that Patricia could think about moving to work in Mohammed's remote mountain town. And what a welcome she and Farnham received when they went to find a suitable house for her to live in.

'Did you enjoy the fish stew?' asked Mohammed's mother, when they had eaten big platefuls of her home cooking.

'Yes, thank you. It was lovely,' her visitors replied.

The older woman smiled and then produced more food.

'This is good mutton stew,' she said.

Farnham had room for mutton stew, but Patricia was struggling.

'Did you enjoy the mutton stew?' asked Mohammed's mother, when they had finished eating.

'Yes, thank you,' her visitors replied, hoping nothing else was to follow.

'Now here's some tasty chicken stew,' she said, placing two more plates down in front of them.

Taking little spoonfuls, her guests ate as much as they possibly could, hoping that there was not yet another stew to follow. There wasn't!

Three months later Patricia moved to the mountain town along with Evelyn, a friend from England who had come on a short visit. The house they lived in was just two little whitewashed rooms with barred windows, but it had a stairway up to a flat roof.

'Look at the view!' Evelyn said, when they climbed up on to the roof. 'It's magnificent.'

A week later, when the first heavy rain fell, Patricia and her friend were at the market.

'Goodness me!' they said together, when they arrived back home.

Water was lapping on the floors of both rooms and the cooking pans floated like little boats!

'There's nothing to stop the rain running right down the stairs! It's open to the sky at the top,' she laughed. 'I should have thought of that!'

The two women enjoyed their three weeks together. But when her friend left, Patricia felt a little scared of being in the house on her own. But on the very first night she read these words from the Bible, 'I, the Lord, watch over it … I guard it day and night so that no-one may harm it.' All her fears went away as she realised that God was looking over her in her little house even when she was fast asleep.

'What's that?' Patricia asked herself one evening a short time later. 'There's someone at the door.'

'Hello,' she said to the little boy who had knocked. 'What can I do for you?'

'Will you give me some bread? I'm hungry,' he replied.

Cutting a thick slice of bread, she gave it to the lad. The following night there was another knock at the door.

'Hello!' Patricia laughed. 'You've brought some friends with you. You'd better all come in.'

Spreading golden syrup on to thick slices of bread, she gave them to her visitors. The boys had never tasted golden syrup before and they licked every last sticky drop from their filthy hands.

'Tell me about yourselves,' she said, when they had finished.

'We're orphans,' one told her.

Another added, 'We don't have homes. We just live on the streets.'

'I'm a good beggar!' a third one boasted.

Before they left that night Patricia told them a Bible story. And every night after that the boys – an increasing number of them – arrived at her door after dark, ate a feast of bread and golden syrup and then listened carefully to a Bible story.

Morocco is a Muslim country, and the teachers at the mosque grew suspicious of Patricia, guessing that she was telling the boys about Jesus. They forbade the children to visit her, and they didn't, for all of three or four nights. Then there was a quiet knock at the door.

'I wonder if they're back,' Patricia said to herself as she rose to answer.

Opening the door just a little bit to see who was there, it was pushed wide from the outside and a whole pile of boys dashed in, shoving it shut behind them. But when the boys left later that night they were attacked by men with sticks. Only one came back after that, and he turned out not to be an orphan at all. Patricia discovered that when he invited his story-telling friend home to meet his family!

A male doctor came to the town three times a week but Muslim men were not happy to have a man looking after their wives and children. As a result women and children didn't have anyone to whom they could go when they were ill. Because the teachers in the mosque knew Patricia was a Christian they didn't want their families to go to her either, even though they knew she was a nurse. One day, when the newborn baby of a rich family became ill, the mother sent her servant to ask Patricia for help. She went and, with God's help, was able to save the little one's life. After that she had more than enough patients coming to her door. She was very grateful when, the following summer, Marguerite came from Switzerland to help her in the work.

'Hello,' said Patricia, 'come on in.'

Tamoo, who was about seven years old, grinned and entered the house.

'You said you would teach me to knit,' she said. 'So I've come to learn.'

The next day Tamoo brought two friends, and the following day she brought some more.

'It's not easy teaching children to knit,' Marguerite laughed, when they had left for the day. 'The wool gets in such a tangle.'

'I know,' her friend agreed. 'But have you realised what we've just started?'

Marguerite looked puzzled.

'We've started a school for girls,' laughed Patricia. 'We have our first pupils and I'm quite sure more will come when they hear about it. I think we should teach them reading and writing as well as knitting. And I think they need fed here too. Have you noticed how thin they are?'

'Yes,' Marguerite agreed. 'The poor girls look half starved.'

Before long there was so much work to do between the girls' school and sick patients that help was needed, and Tamoo's mother was that help. Fatima came every day and very soon Patricia couldn't do without her.

One day Fatima arrived in a very great state of upset.

'My husband and his new wife have taken Tamoo away to be their servant,' she said. 'And he says I can't have her back again.'

Fatima's husband was not a good man, and he wouldn't let Tamoo see her mum unless they met at the well. Weeks passed and poor Fatima grew very sad because she missed her little daughter so much.

'Who's that?' Patricia asked late one night, when there was a sharp knock on the door.

As she unlocked the door it was pushed open from outside and Fatima staggered in carrying Tamoo in her arms. She was nearly dead with pneumonia. Patricia examined the little girl as her mother told her story.

'Somebody told me that Tamoo was ill and I couldn't sleep for thinking about her. Then, as I tossed and turned, the Lord Jesus spoke into my heart and I knew that I had to go and rescue her. So I went through the streets, hiding in the shadows when anyone came, and arrived at the door of my husband's house. I waited for a long time outside because I thought he would chase me away. But I couldn't go away because I could hear Tamoo crying and coughing inside. Then I opened the door … and the house was empty apart from my daughter. So I wrapped her in a blanket and ran all the way here.'

Not long afterwards Fatima trusted in the Lord Jesus Christ as her Saviour.

Women began to gather in Patricia's house to hear stories of Jesus and to drink cups of mint tea. One was called Zorah, and she was Fatima's mother. Although Zorah was an elderly woman she worked as a water carrier, which was a very hard job indeed.

'Today I want to tell you about some words of Jesus,'

said Patricia in Arabic to her women friends. 'Jesus said, "Come to me, all you who are weary and burdened, and I will give you rest" (Matthew 11: 28). Because Zorah knew that she was often tired and weary, and she knew that her water jars were heavy burdens, she believed that God's Word was speaking right to her. That was the first step in her journey to becoming a Christian.

'Well I never!' laughed Patricia, as she unpacked a parcel from England. 'Someone has sent a whole bundle of things, including a clockwork mouse for the children to play with.'

The next day, after lessons, she gave the mouse to the girls and they had a wonderful time.

'Why are so many women coming to the meeting?' she wondered a few days later, when the door was knocked over and over and over and over again. After the Bible story none of the women rose to go home.

'Do you want to hear another story?' asked the missionary.

'No,' one of the women giggled. 'Please may we see the running-around mouse!'

Patricia laughed heartily. 'So that's why you've all come!'

She produced the clockwork mouse, wound it up and placed it on the floor. It ran across the room and the women laughed and screamed and had every bit as good a time as the children!

Mountain Villages

'We can't have a meeting for the women tomorrow,' Patricia said to Fatima one day. 'I need to go on a journey.'

'Can't we still have a meeting?' she was asked.

'But I won't be here to tell the Bible story.'

Fatima shook her head. 'We can still sing to the Lord and pray. And we remember the Bible stories you've told us and we can talk about them.'

The next day, as Patricia left on her journey, she thanked God that although she was not there her Christian friend Fatima would continue to talk to the town's women about Jesus. It was a Muslim town, and the teachers at the mosque would not have been at all pleased if they'd known what was happening, but Fatima held the meetings all the same.

Marguerite went back home to Switzerland and Brente, who came from Denmark, arrived in the town to help Patricia St. John with her work. The children loved Brente and she loved working with them, which meant that Patricia had enough time to begin writing another book. For a while she had been far too busy even to think about writing. **Star of Light** is about life in a mountain town just like that one, and it was about people just like the people she met day by day.

'Do you think you could help this boy?' Mohammed asked, dragging a frightened lad into the house after him. 'His name's Hamid.'

Patricia looked at he boy. His head was shaved, he was battered and bruised, and he had a horrible sore that ran almost from his knee to his ankle.

'Would you let me wash your sore leg?' asked Patricia. 'I'll try hard not to hurt you.'

Hamid dashed to the opposite corner of the room. He certainly was not going to let her near him. Patricia prepared cotton wool and clean water in a bowl. She knew about children, and had worked out how to help Hamid.

'Here's cotton wool and water,' she said. 'I'll stay in this corner, you stay in your corner and I'll tell you what to do.'

Hamid did what he was told, even though his leg was terribly sore.

'Would you let me bandage it?' Patricia said, but the boy looked as though he was going to make a run for the door. 'Would you let Mohammed help you to bandage it then?'

He nodded his head and, with Mohammed's help, the leg was bandaged without the missionary ever laying hands on him. Hamid did let Patricia pray for him and ask the Lord to make his leg better. God answered that prayer. By the time his leg was better, Hamid had joined the group of boys who were once again coming to the house after dark. Night after night they ate together and listened to Bible stories.

By then Patricia had been in the town so long that women knew where to come for help when they or their children were sick. Soon even those living in the villages round about heard that there was a nurse in town and they started to come to see her too. Eventually she was asked to go out to the villages to hold small clinics so that sick people didn't need to travel to see her.

'What do we need to take with us?' Brente asked, as they prepared for their first village clinic.

'Pack iron pills for the mothers, some worm tablets, gentian violet for sores, and ointment for eye infections,' the missionary nurse replied. 'And we'd better take some malt for the children too and sulphur tablets for children who are sick and have runny tummies.'

Before many weeks had passed there was a queue of people waiting in villages by the time Brente and Patricia arrived, so many that they couldn't see them all on one day.

'Will you stay overnight?' they were asked, after that had happened once or twice.

The two women looked at each other and decided that they would stay. After they had seen their last patient for the day, and had eaten a simple meal, they sat with the village women and Patricia told them Bible stories.

'I like the one about the shepherd looking for his lost sheep,' a woman said at the end of the evening. 'He was a good shepherd.'

Patricia smiled. 'The Lord Jesus is the best shepherd of all,' she told her. 'And those who trust in him are his lambs, and he loves every single one of them.'

The woman looked thoughtful. 'I hope you'll tell us more about him next time you come.'

The months passed and Patricia and Brente went many miles to distant villages to treat the sick and to tell people about Jesus.

'I'm really sorry to be leaving,' Brente said, when her time in Morocco was nearly over. 'But Fatima is a good teacher now. She'll be a great help to you.'

Brente was quite right. Even before she left, Fatima was invited by a woman called Yamana to go to her village.

'Will you and Fatima teach us about the Lord?' she said to Patricia.

The missionary was delighted!

'You could stay overnight.'

It took a little working out, but eventually Fatima and Patricia – with Tamoo, of course - went to Yamana's village on Monday afternoons. They came back early on Tuesdays to be ready for school - a three hour walk each way that crossed over a deep river. While the villagers liked hearing Patricia speaking, what they liked best was when Fatima told them the stories that Jesus had told when he was on earth.

'Remember that it's the Muslim feast of Ramadan,' Fatima told her friend before she set off one day. 'So you won't get anything to eat between early morning and late evening.'

In fact Patricia was sound asleep under the stars by the time the night meal was made.

'Wake up!' a village woman said, 'I've made a feast and you are our special guest.'

Rubbing her eyes, Patricia sat up and looked around. There was indeed a feast spread and everyone had gathered to eat. She looked at her plate and discovered a little dish of cooked goats' eyes were waiting to be eaten by the family's special guest!

Dr Farnham went to visit his sister in her mountain town once a month and he treated any patients who had serious problems. Sometimes he took visitors from abroad with him and they clung to his back as Farnham's motor bike drove round hairpin bends with steep drops on one side!

'Do you go to the villages in turn?' a visitor asked Patricia one day.

She shook her head. 'No,' she said. 'We never ever go without being invited. You see, the people are really kind to us if they invite us to their village. But if a missionary went without an invitation, she might be treated very harshly indeed. There are prickly pear fences around the villages with guard dogs trained to keep the people safe from unwelcome visitors. If I were to go without an invitation, I could easily find the guard dogs being let loose on me.'

'That could be very dangerous,' said the visitor, who was also a doctor. 'Not only could you be bitten, but dogs like that can carry dangerous diseases too.'

Smiling, Patricia assured him that she only ever went to villages by invitation as she had no intention of being bitten by a bad-tempered dog, whether or not it was infectious!

'We've never been to that village,' Fatima said, pointing to a settlement high on the hills.

'I know,' agreed Patricia, 'and the people there have probably never heard about the Lord Jesus.'

'We'll pray that God will make someone there invite us to visit,' her friend suggested. 'And we'll keep praying about it until it happens.'

One day, when Patricia, Fatima and Tamoo were on their long walk back from Yamana's village, a bus came along.

'Let's catch it!' said Patricia. 'We'll get home quicker that way.'

All three climbed aboard and the rickety bus set off.

'Will you please stop at the end of the road that leads to our town?' Fatima asked the driver, who was not in a good mood at all.

'No,' he grumped. 'That's not an official bus stop. And the next official stop is five or six miles away!'

Patricia and Fatima looked at each other, shrugged their shoulders, and sat down again.

'We're not going to be home early at all,' grumbled Patricia, 'because we'll have to walk all the way back now.' By then she wasn't in a very good mood either!

Fatima looked round at her friend.

'Why are you grumbling?' she asked. 'We asked God to guide us today so he must be wanting us down in the valley.'

Feeling very guilty for being so cross, Patricia smiled and agreed that Fatima was right and she was wrong. When the bus eventually stopped, it was at the corner of the road that led all the way up to the village on the other side of valley, the village for which they had been praying.

They were only off the bus a few minutes when a woman's voice called out behind them.

'Excuse me!' it said politely.

Patricia, Fatima and little Tamoo turned round. There was a woman behind them, and Muslim women didn't usually go out alone. In fact, they hardly ever did that.

'Is that the nurse from England?' the woman asked Fatima, speaking in the local language.

'Yes it is,' she was told.

'I want to speak to her then. Please introduce us.'

Fatima did that and then the woman pulled back a cloth from the bundle she was carrying and there was a very poorly baby! The little one had a terrible eye infection, the worst Patricia had ever seen.

'Why didn't you bring the baby to me earlier?' she asked the young mother.

The woman looked surprised.

'I didn't know about you earlier,' she explained. 'Last night I was so worried about my baby and a voice told me to take him to the English nurse. I said that I didn't know an English nurse. Then the voice told me to go down to the corner of the road and wait for the English nurse to come. So this morning I came down and waited for you.'

As they climbed the five miles up the mountain road to the town to get medicine for the baby, Patricia and Fatima thanked God that he had answered their prayers and that the bus driver didn't let them off at their road's end!

After the baby's eyes had been treated the two friends were invited to visit the mother's village!

'Let's take the wordless book with us,' the women decided, as they prepared for their Saturday climb.

Fatima smiled. 'It's a wonderful book,' she said. 'All it has is different coloured pages. It has no words at all but it says such a lot about Jesus.'

When they arrived at the village the baby's eyes were

looking better and the villagers were so pleased about it that they gave the visitors a wonderful welcome.

'Let me tell you about the wordless book,' Fatima said, as the women gathered to drink mint tea.

Turning the pages of the little book, she told the story.

'This gold page tells us about heaven, a bright and beautiful place to which you can go if you believe in Jesus. God lives in the golden heaven. The black page tells us about sin that makes our hearts hard and black. If our hearts are black with sin we can't go to the beautiful heaven. Now we come to the red page. This page tells us that God sent his Son, the Lord Jesus, to die on a cross, to shed his red blood, to take away the blackness of our sinful hearts. The white page shows us how clean and white our hearts are after Jesus has taken away all our sins. And the green page tells us that after we believe and have our hearts washed clean we have to learn about the Lord Jesus so that we can grow like green plants, growing more like him every day. And that brings us back to the golden page, because everyone whose sins are forgiven goes to heaven when they die. And in heaven they will meet the Lord Jesus face to face.'

One of the village women, who had listened to every single word Fatima said, took Patricia's hand and walked a little way down the steep path with the visitors.

'Could I have that book?' she asked. 'I can't read words but I could read the colours and learn about God every day.'

Fatima gave her the book and the village woman climbed back up the hill to her home.

Sad Goodbye

The women from the mountain village asked Patricia and Fatima to visit them again and again, and they were pleased to do so.

'Is there anyone who can stop me from losing my temper and telling lies?' they were asked one day, as they packed up their medicines.

'Only Jesus can do that,' Fatima told the mother who has asked the question.

The villager looked astonished.

'Your Jesus can do that!' she said. 'Next time you come you'll have to tell me how he does it.'

Patricia was sure that the young mother really wanted to ask more that day, but some men were standing close by and the women were not as relaxed as usual. Instead of walking a little way down the hill with their visitors, the mothers said a quick thank you for their medical help and wished them a good journey home.

'I think the men are causing trouble,' Fatima said, when they were out of earshot. 'I wouldn't be surprised if we're not asked back again for a while.'

Patricia's heart filled with sadness. How she wished she had been able to tell the woman that she needed

71

to trust in the Lord Jesus if he was to help her to keep her temper and not tell lies.

'That will be the boys,' Patricia St. John smiled as she rose to open the door late one night. 'They'll be pleased to see that Farnham brought out a large tin of golden syrup when he came to do the clinic today. It's really useful having him come up here every month! He's good at shopping as well as doctoring!'

The boys slid in quickly and silently, and one stayed on the street as a look-out.

'What's wrong?' their missionary friend asked, seeing their serious faces.

She had hardly said the words when news seemed to tumble out of the boys. Patricia had to listen very hard for they all spoke at once and they talked in whispers.

'We were questioned in the market place today.'

'I was asked if you told us about Jesus.'

'The teacher from the mosque beat me when I said you were my friend,' one said, holding out a sore bruised arm to prove that what he was saying was true.

'We've been told not to come here ever again.'

'You're going to be sent away,' a thin hungry boy said. 'Who'll feed us if you go away?'

His little brother looked deep into Patricia's eyes. 'Who'll love us if you go away?' he asked sadly.

Shocked at what she was hearing, the missionary realised that there was serious trouble brewing.

'Let's eat and talk,' she told them.

The boys seemed to relax at the thought of food, though they hardly noticed the new tin of golden syrup.

'Was it soldiers who beat you?' Patricia asked. 'Or was it just older boys being bullies?'

'It was the soldiers,' she was told. 'And two of the teachers from the mosque were standing there watching and laughing.'

'Please be careful,' the missionary told her beloved scamps. 'I don't want you to be hurt.'

The oldest boy spoke for them all, and spoke bravely. 'We'll be careful,' he said. 'But we'll not stop coming, and we'll take turns at being look-out.'

Just as he said the words, there was a sharp knock at the door.

'That's the signal,' the same boy said. 'Ali must have heard footsteps in the distance. Run for it!'

Within seconds the room was empty apart from Patricia, who rushed to clear away any signs of her visitors. Then she climbed up the stair on to her roof and crept to where she could see what was happening below. There wasn't a boy to be seen, but a soldier was standing just outside her house. As she didn't dare move until he went away, she sat where she was and prayed for her brave young friends.

The whole atmosphere in the town began to change. Until then Patricia had felt safe, if sometimes unwelcome, but now she found herself looking around to see who was behind her, and sticking to busy parts of town rather than walking down lonely lanes.

'I must buy some fruit,' she thought, after visiting a patient at home. 'I'll go by the market on my way home.'

'Ouch! You're hurting me!' she heard a child scream, as she paid for her fruit.

Patricia spun round and saw that a soldier had grabbed one of the girls who came to her school, and was twisting her arm up her back! Patricia ran to the soldier, who loosened his grip just a little when he realised who she was.

'Please set that little girl free,' the missionary said. 'She's only a child!'

The soldier gave the child's arm a really sore tug up her back and then pushed her away roughly. As soon as she was free she ran into Patricia's arms. It took the child a long time to be able to speak, for she had thought she was going to be taken away to prison.

'He told me not to go back to your school,' she sobbed eventually.

'I thought he might have said that,' said Patricia sadly. 'And I think you should have a holiday for a week.'

The little girl grinned in surprise.

'In fact,' Patricia whispered, 'you run round the town and tell all the pupils they can have a holiday for a week.'

As she made her way back home the missionary's heart was full of sadness.

'I've been free to work here for five years,' she thought. 'But it looks as though it is now coming to an end. I wouldn't be surprised if I'm the next one to have a soldier knocking on my door.'

Patricia was absolutely right.

'You are to come down to the police station,' she was told, when she answered the door a few days later. 'They want you for questioning.'

Praying quietly as she prepared for the interview, Patricia asked the Lord to give her the right words to say.

'Please sit down,' the Inspector told her, when she arrived at the police station.

He shuffled through a file of papers that was lying on his desk.

'It's about your visa …' he announced, lifting up an official looking form.

'Because I'm British I don't need a visa,' said Patricia.

He put the paper down.

'Oh … yes … of course.'

The man searched through his papers again until he found the one he was looking for.

'There have been complaints made about you to the police,' he said.

'Have I broken any law?' Patricia asked politely.

The Inspector ignored her question.

'It seems that you've been visiting the high village on the other side of the valley. Is that true?'

'We were asked by a young mother to treat her baby's eye infection.'

The man was becoming impatient.

'Is it true that you've been visiting the high village on the other side of the valley?' he demanded.

'That is true,' agreed the missionary.

'Please do not go there again,' she was told. 'We are watching what you are doing. Now, you may go.'

As she closed the door behind her, Patricia knew that the day would soon come when she would be asked to leave her mountain home.

For a few weeks life returned to normal. Then one day Fatima, flushed and excited, arrived for work.

'I had a dream last night,' she told Patricia. 'And I'm sure God was speaking to me through it.'

'What did you dream about?' her friend enquired.

Fatima sat down and got her breath back; she had rushed through the streets to get there.

'I dreamed that I was walking beside a stream when, quite suddenly, the stream became so full of water that it burst its banks and carried me away. I felt as if I was drowning. It was very frightening. Then someone in a white robe, who was standing on the dry ground at the side of the rushing water, reached out and pulled me on to dry land.'

There was silence as the two women thought about the dream.

'I'm sure that some great trouble is going to come,' said Fatima quietly. 'But Jesus will help us through it.'

'I wonder where Fatima is,' thought Patricia a few weeks later. 'She's not often late in coming. I think I'll walk along the road to meet her.'

She had just passed the market place when she saw Fatima and her family being taken into the courthouse by the police! Patricia walked on.

'I mustn't show the police that I recognise my friend,' she thought. 'I'll just glance at her once and hope our eyes meet.'

And when Patricia dared to look up, she and Fatima looked into each other's eyes for a split second. As she turned to go in the door of the courthouse Fatima pointed towards heaven.

'She knows that God will look after her,' the missionary decided. 'And he will.'

By evening Patricia had heard nothing from Fatima and she set out through the streets to the courthouse to see what was happening. Having prayed what she should do, she was sure it was right that she go.

'I will take you to the Governor of the City,' the official told her when she went in the door.

'Please will you sit down,' said the Governor politely. 'I know that you have come because this family are your friends. But from now on they must never go

77

to your house. And you must stop all Christian teaching. I am going to order a guard to be set at the end of your street and if these people, or any other people, visit you they will be beaten and put in prison.'

It was several days before anyone dared visit Patricia, and even then her friends came late at night, or even during the night. But she knew things could not go on. She had no patients as people were afraid to go to her for help. The school was closed because it was far too dangerous for girls to attend. The City Governor could see that there was no reason for her to stay, and Patricia could see it too. Her only comfort was that there were two lady missionaries living a short distance outside of the town and she prayed that somehow those who wanted to know about the Lord Jesus would find a way to ask them their questions.

Patricia smiled when a letter arrived from Farnham. Somehow he always seemed to say just the right thing. She made herself a cup of mint tea and then sat down and slit the envelope open. After the first few lines she found herself reading aloud. Perhaps she had been on her own for too long! 'I think you should come back to Tangier,' Farnham wrote, 'and I have an idea of what you can do here. As you know it's very dangerous for young Christian girls who stay in their own towns and villages. It's even difficult for any who would like to know about the Lord to ask, because they know they'll be seen speaking to a missionary, and that's just not safe these days.' Patricia looked up from the letter. 'How true that is,' she thought, before continuing to read. 'If you come back to Tangier, you could start a nursing school for girls. Missionaries could let us know of suitable girls and we could look after them in Tangier. They would study nursing, of course, but you could also do Bible studies with them as part of their training. That would be a safe way for them to learn about the Lord.'

As Patricia needed time to think and time to plan she went back to England to spend Christmas with her family.

'I don't know where you found the time to write since you went to Morocco,' her aunt said. 'I've read the three children's books you wrote there: **Three Go Searching**, **The Fourth Candle** and **Star of Light**. They're very good!'

Her niece laughed. 'I don't understand how you find time to read!'

Patricia, knowing that her aunt was headmistress of a splendid school, was pleased to hear that her books were thought to be good.

From England the missionary then went to Egypt to learn how to train village girls to be nurses, especially girls who had very little education. And after two months there she was quite sure Farnham was right.

It was a good idea to open a nursing school for village girls who were interested in the Lord. But there was something she had to do first. She had to go back to her mountain home to say goodbye to her friends and to collect her things. With a sad heart she set off, wondering what had happened to her boys and her schoolgirls since she left.

Just a short time later she was back in Tangier, full of news for her brother and his wife.

'I can hardly believe how things have worked out,' she told them. 'Fatima is teaching the children in her own house! "My boys" are being looked after by a Christian couple. And the local Christians are going to the lady missionaries who live outside the town and they are still learning more about the Lord.'

'So you don't feel so bad about leaving,' Farnham suggested, knowing that was only half true.

His sister smiled sadly. 'My head tells me that God will care for his people up in the mountains,' she said. 'But my heart tells me that I'm going to miss them more than words can tell. If you had seen the boys' faces when I left them, you would know why I left with a very sad heart.'

No Veils!

Patricia looked round the room and smiled at the seven teenaged girls who had just arrived. Most were Moroccans and one or two were from Algeria.

'This will be your home,' she said, 'and I'll share it with you. Dar Scott is a lovely big house and I hope you'll be happy here while you're doing your nursing training.'

As most were from mountain villages, Dar Scott was very different from any house the girls had ever been in before.

'Let me tell you what you'll be doing,' went on Patricia. 'As you know you've all been specially chosen to train as nurses here in the hospital at Tangier. Until now nearly all hospitals have only had male nurses and you are going to be among the first female nurses in the country.'

'Won't people think it's strange to have girls nursing them?' one of them asked.

Patricia nodded. 'I'm quite sure they will,' she said. 'But I want you to be such good nurses that they'll like being nursed by you. You are real trailblazers and I've no doubt that there will be many more young women who'll follow in your footsteps over the years.'

The girls smiled shyly at each other. Patricia made them feel special. In fact, one of her gifts was that she made whoever she was with feel special.

'You're going to be busy,' Patricia St. John told her students over their meal that evening. 'You'll study anatomy, physiology, nursing skills and, of course, the Bible. And that's a really good mixture of subjects.'

Seeing puzzled looks on several faces, she went on. 'Anatomy and physiology will teach you how the human body is made and how it works. In the Bible we'll learn about the Lord God Almighty who knows how the human body works because he made everyone who has ever lived. Nursing skills will show you how to care for someone who is sick and how best to help them get better. The Bible teaches us how much the Lord cares for those he has made and what he did to save his people from the sickness of sin. That's why I say that nursing and the Bible go very well together.'

Although the girls agreed, most of them were still too nervous to say much to Patricia. They were just fifteen and sixteen years old and shy of strangers, especially strangers from a foreign land. All had been chosen for nursing training by missionaries who knew them and who felt they had an interest in the Christian faith. Although at first they were shy of Patricia, they had a much more serious situation in which they had to overcome their shyness before they could be of any use in the wards.

'But I've never met a strange man when I've had my veil off,' one of them said a little nervously. 'Won't the men think I'm doing wrong?' she asked.

Patricia understood the problem. 'I know you all cover your faces in the presence of men as that is the custom in Morocco. I know that men disapprove of women who don't wear the veil, but they will just have to get used to that. Patients must see your faces when you nurse them. You can wear your veils when you're off-duty.'

'My father says I can only be unveiled in the ward if there's a senior nurse there,' an Algerian student said. 'Otherwise he says I've to go right back home.'

'We've explained to your parents that there will always be a senior nurse on with you anyway,' Patricia smiled. 'You don't think we'd leave you in a ward all by yourself, do you?'

The girl relaxed. 'I'd be terrified if you did!' she laughed. 'I wouldn't know what to do if someone took very ill!'

Her teacher patted her on the shoulder. 'By the time you've finished your training you'll know what to do in an emergency. But, first things first. What are the names of the bones in the leg, starting from the bottom and working up?'

'The two lower leg bones are the tibia and fibula,' said the first student.

Her friend took over. 'Then there's the knee-cap, or patella.'

'Which takes us up to the femur,' added the next girl, 'which goes into a ball and socket joint at the hip.'

Patricia smiled. 'Well done!' she said. 'You really listened to today's lesson. I hope you'll listen as well tomorrow.'

That evening Patricia went to her brother's house to spend some time with him and his family. When she returned to Dar Scott the girls, who were relaxing in the sitting room, suddenly changed the subject and started talking about leg bones! She just caught the change as she opened the door to go in, but she heard enough to know that the girls thought they were working too hard.

'Do any of you know how to do charades?' she asked.

Her students looked up. Was this something else they had to learn before they went to bed, they wondered. Patricia smiled. They really hadn't understood that they could relax and play together as well as work together.

'I'll show you,' she said. 'Guess what my job is.'

Patricia pretended to carry a wooden bucket and set it on the ground. Then she squatted down beside it and made squeezing movements with her hands. One of the girls giggled.

'You're pretending to milk a goat!' she said.

And all seven burst into loud laughter.

'Now one of you try to mime a job and we'll see if we can guess what it is.'

The oldest mimed being a water-carrier and it took three guesses for her friends to get it right. By the time the game of charades was over, all the student nurses had learned that Patricia was their friend as well as their teacher. And when she opened her Bible to take evening prayers they all listened very carefully to what their new friend had to say about the verses they read together.

'This is Milk Clinic day,' Patricia told the girls the following morning. 'And I'd like you all to come along to see the work we're doing there. But first, let me explain how we measure and record a child's growth.'

Pointing to a chart on the wall, she explained that the space between the top and bottom lines on the chart showed the normal weight of growing babies, and that the figures along the bottom showed the baby's age in weeks.

'Now let's see if you understand. What weight should a baby be at six weeks if it weighed three and a quarter kilos when it was born?'

She had explained the chart well and all her students gave the correct answer.

Patricia smiled. 'Let's do one more. What weight should a baby be at four months if it weighted two and three quarter kilos when it was born?'

Once again everyone gave the correct answer.

'Well done,' said their teacher. 'But I'm afraid that most of the babies you'll see at the clinic will be well below the weight they should be, which is why we give their mothers powdered milk formula and vitamins for them. Why do you think these babies are underweight?' she asked.

'A mother might have had another baby and there's not enough milk for both,' suggested the youngest girl. She knew a lot about new babies as she had five younger brothers and sisters.

'That's the most common reason,' Patricia agreed.

Another student raised her hand.

'Is it because their mothers are not having enough to eat themselves?' she asked.

Their teacher nodded her head.

'And when there's not enough mother's milk for a baby what are they fed?' she asked.

All the hands went up.

'Bread soaked in mint tea,' they said. They'd all seen this fed to little children in their own villages.

'I'm afraid there's not enough goodness in bread and mint tea to help a child grow. Many of those you'll see today have come in suffering from malnutrition because of being fed on bread soaked in mint tea.'

Many mothers brought their babies to the clinic that morning.

'Look at that poor child,' one student said to another. 'His arms and legs are very thin.'

Her friend looked away, sad at the sight of the little boy. Held in his mother's arms, the baby took very little interest in what was happening around him.

'Let's weigh you,' Patricia said, lifting him on to the scales. 'I think this is your first visit to the clinic so you don't have a card.'

She put the boy's name on a card and then wrote down his weight.

'Where does he fit on the chart?' she asked her students.

But the boy didn't fit on the chart at all. At least, he didn't fit in between the lines of normal weight. In fact, he was so underweight that he was right at the bottom of the chart.

'Please bring him back to the clinic next week,' Patricia told the boy's mother, as she handed her powdered baby formula and vitamin drops. 'We should see a difference in him by then.'

The following week the young mother brought her son back to be weighed. He was still very thin, but his eyes were brighter and he watched what was happening around him. Within just a few weeks the nursing students were delighted to see him looking like an ordinary little boy.

'Will this be his last visit to the clinic?' one of them asked Patricia. 'His weight is normal on the chart now.'

'If we made this his last visit,' her teacher explained, 'it wouldn't be long until he was underweight again. No, we'll keep him coming back for several months and provide him with milk and vitamins until he's really built up and strong.'

One day a mother arrived with a very sick infant in her arms.

'I think you should leave the baby in hospital with us,' she was told.

The poor woman wouldn't do that as she was afraid her daughter would die and she wouldn't be there to cuddle her.

'Just give me medicine and I'll go away. I've other children to look after and goats to milk.'

One of the nurses, her name was Janet, suggested that the mother stay until the heat went out of the sun before walking the long way home. 'And if you do, I can give your baby medicine by injection while you're here.'

The mother agreed and spent all day in the cool of the missionary's living room. Each time Janet gave the little girl medicine, she talked to the woman about the Lord Jesus. By the time the sun began to fade, her baby was a little better and the woman had a longing to hear about Jesus. She came back to the hospital over and again to learn more about the Lord and came to love him as her Saviour. Then for some weeks the young mother didn't appear at all.

'Her new baby will have come,' Janet told Patricia. 'I hope she and the baby are all right.'

One day, not very long afterwards, the Moroccan lady arrived at the hospital.

'Why didn't you tell me what would happen?' she asked the missionaries. 'Why didn't you warn me?'

It took some time to find out what the matter was. After she trusted in the Lord Jesus Christ the young woman had told her family and friends about him. Those she spoke to were very suspicious and wouldn't have anything to do with her!

'Even when my new baby was born my mother wouldn't come to help,' she said sadly. 'Why didn't you tell me that would happen?'

Patricia sat beside the poor woman for a while before speaking.

'Do you think you made a mistake to believe in Jesus?' she asked quietly.

The young mother turned and stared at her.

'A mistake?' she said. 'No! Never! Never, never, never!!!'

Very quietly Patricia explained that those who are forgiven through the Lord Jesus Christ have to forgive those who hurt them.

'But ... but I can't forgive them!' she said, thinking of what her own mother had done.

Slowly and gently the missionary explained that Christians have no choice. They have to forgive those who hurt them. After what seemed like a very long time the young woman picked up her tiny baby, cuddled him in her arms and said, 'I will forgive them. I will go home and do them good.'

When Patricia looked back over her time in Morocco she felt both joy and sadness.

'There's so much to be thankful for,' she thought. 'People have become Christians in their ones and twos. It's such a big step for them because they meet opposition in their homes and villages. I'm especially thankful that some of the girls who have come here to study nursing have become members of the little church in Tangier and they are faithfully following the Lord.' She smiled as she thought of the girls and of the happy and busy times they had had together. 'But there are others,' she remembered sadly, 'who looked as though they were following Jesus but they've fallen away now.' Then a surprising thought came into her mind. 'That happened to Jesus too! Some people who heard him believed and followed the Lord. Others heard and seemed to believe but they went back to their old ways. Jesus remembers what that feels like and he knows and understands how I feel today.'

Dad

'That was a strange dream,' thought Patricia, when she woke up from a restless night's sleep.

She had dreamed that her father was lying on the ground reaching out to her, but she couldn't stretch far enough to help him. Later that day a telegram arrived bringing news of Mr St. John.

'Dad has had a severe heart attack,' it read. 'I don't think he's likely to live for very long.'

Arrangements were made for another missionary to come to look after the girls who were training to be nurses, and Patricia quickly packed to go home. She had to think what to take with her as it was September and, if she stayed some months in England, she would need her winter clothes. So it was that in 1956 she found herself unexpectedly back in the UK, much to the relief of her mother and to her father's delight. Although he was very poorly indeed, he was still glad to see his daughter. Over the months that followed the pair of them spent a great deal of time together.

'Was it terribly hard for you all,' Father asked one day, 'when I left you in England and went back to South America?'

Patricia didn't answer right away. It was a question that needed some thought.

'I don't think it was,' she said a minute or two later. 'Of course we missed you a lot but Holmesdale was such a busy house and always so full of people.'

Dad smiled. 'I suppose it was,' he agreed. 'There was Great-grandmother, Grandmother, Mum and all of you children, not to mention the brave Elsie down there in the kitchen.'

'You've no idea how much we looked forward to your visits home,' Patricia told her father. 'For weeks we seemed to talk about nothing else. We'd try to work out what to show you first and what to tell you first. Once we even worked out the order in which we'd speak to you! But when you did arrive we forgot our plans and all spoke at once!'

Patricia laughed warmly. 'Do you remember the time you came earlier than expected and met one of the village girls out walking John in his pram. You thought the baby looked like one of the family and asked her if he was.'

'Really,' Dad said softly. 'What on earth did I say?'

'The girl told me later,' Patricia answered. 'Apparently you said, "Excuse me, but could you possibly tell me … is this by any chance my baby?" The girl, who had never seen you before, replied, "I'm sure I couldn't possibly say, sir," and wheeled John off in a great hurry!'

Mr St. John smiled broadly. 'Imagine me being silly

enough to do that when I'd never seen the girl before. But it was so good to see you after my long times away I just couldn't wait for her to bring John home from his walk to say a proper hello to him.'

'Was it hard for you not to see us?' Patricia asked. It was a question about which she'd often wondered, but had never before asked.

'Yes, it was,' her father replied. 'The day before I left home was worst of all. Your mother and I believed we were doing what the Lord wanted us to do, but it was so hard to visit you all in your bedrooms after you were asleep and to know that I wouldn't do that again for a very long time. I loved the feel of your warm breath on my hand as I stroked each of your faces, and the nuzzling noises you all made in your sleep. I used to go from bed to bed praying that the Lord would keep you in his care while I was away from home. And he did.'

'I think it's time you slept,' suggested Patricia. 'That old heart of yours needs plenty of rest these days.'

As she patted his pillows into comfortable softness, her father smiled. 'Will you stay and feel my warm breath on your hands and listen to my nuzzling noises?' he teased.

His daughter laughed heartily.

'Mother and I can hear you snoring from next door!' she said.

That night, as Patricia lay in bed thinking about her father, she remembered the letters he had written to her. He wrote short letters to each of his children, but he wrote regularly and they all looked forward to receiving them.

'Dad said in letters what many fathers wouldn't even say face-to-face to their children,' she thought. 'I remember once when I was working out in the villages and the government wanted to stop what we were doing, I wrote and told Dad what was happening. I still remember his wise reply. He said that if God sent us to work in a different place he was well able to look after the people we left behind.'

With that letter in her mind Patricia drifted off to sleep and dreamed of the Christians she had left in the villages. She had no doubt that God cared for them even though she was not there to encourage and help them. The following day her work in the mountains was still on her mind, and Patricia and her father talked about his visit to her in Morocco in 1952. That subject kept them going all day.

Eight months after she received the telegram saying that her father might not live long, he died and went home to his heavenly Father whom he had loved and served. That night Patricia and her mother seemed to have so much to talk about.

'These last four years have been so special,' said Mrs St. John. 'When your father was no longer fit to travel it was a real treat to have him at home with me after all the years of coming and going. Of course, we had this new part of the country to explore in our little walks. And he was chaplain to the school too.'

'It's strange to think of Clarendon School being here in North Wales rather than in Malvern,' commented Patricia. 'And it was lovely of Aunt to give you a flat in the new school when it moved here.'

'Your aunt has always been good to us,' said Mother. 'She has supported us in the Lord's work right from the very beginning. And to think that just a few months ago your father was still teaching Scripture in Clarendon School, that he was still telling the girls about the Lord Jesus.'

Not long after her father's death Patricia had to make some decisions. Should she go right back to Morocco? Should she stay at home for a time with her mother? Eventually the way ahead became clear. She would go back to Morocco for a short time and then return to England to care for her mother when she had eye surgery. When she did return to England a few months later, Patricia's aunt had an idea.

'While you're home, would you consider being matron in Clarendon School?' she asked.

Thinking back to the very happy times she had in the old Malvern Clarendon, Patricia St. John decided that would be a very good thing to do.

'Are you busy, dear?' Mother asked, as she went into Patricia's room on her afternoon off.

The Story behind the Stories

'I'm just trying to plan how to write Father's story,' her daughter said. 'Would you like to help?'

'If I can,' the old lady smiled. 'But I don't want you to put me in the book at all. Remember, it's your father's story you're writing.'

Patricia, who was used to her mother's humility, put down her pen.

'There was a little bit of an age gap between me and your father. In fact, his sister was my governess for a while, so he and I knew each other very well when we were growing up. He used to call me Piglet. If anyone else had called me Piglet, I wouldn't have liked it at all. But he was so gentle that I knew he didn't mean it unkindly. Dad became a Christian when he was nineteen and over the years he prayed for my conversion, for he would never have married someone who didn't love the Lord. He waited patiently until I was a Christian and had nearly finished my studies, and then one day, as we crossed a road together, he asked me to be his wife. Your father worked in the bank then. But before long plans were being made for our wedding, and for us going to Mexico as missionaries!'

'That's a beautiful story,' Patricia told her mother. 'And even though you were separated for many years of your married life he loved you dearly right to the end.'

'And I loved him,' said Mrs St. John. 'But we'll only be apart for a short time now for it can't be too long before God calls me home to heaven too.'

96

God had another home for Mrs St. John before she went to heaven, because after Patricia went back to Morocco in 1965, her mother moved out there to be near her family.

Choose One!

It was a hot day and Patricia was sitting in the shade. There seemed to be children everywhere. Suddenly a boy of about nine ran past and a memory came back to her so freshly it was as though the events had happened just yesterday. Smiling, she let the memory play out like a film in her mind. One day a woman arrived at the hospital with five or six young children. She had been a patient there two years before that and had come to love the Lord Jesus while recovering from an operation. But she was unable to read and write and just longed to discover for herself what the Bible said.

'Do you know me?' she asked.

Patricia and her fellow nurses took a little time to remember. After all, it was a while since she'd been in hospital and so many patients came and went.

'I'm your sister in Christ,' the woman explained. 'The Lord Jesus has washed away my sins. I want you to choose one of my children and keep him here until he can read well enough to come home and read the Bible to me.'

Patricia thought this sounded a very good idea. She looked at the children, some of whom were far too small to learn to read.

'I'll take this one,' she said, choosing a boy of about nine.

Happy at the arrangement that had been made, the woman took her other children and left for the very long walk home to her village.

The boy started school and it seemed he would be a fast learner.

'Are you happy?' Patricia asked, when a week had passed.

'Oh yes!' the nine-year-old answered. 'I'm very happy. But ...'

'What's wrong?' she enquired gently.

'... it's just that I'm cold and lonely at nights. I've never slept all by myself before.'

Patricia smiled. 'Would you like me to take you home for the weekend?'

He did not need to say anything for he was grinning from ear to ear. When Patricia went to collect him on Sunday afternoon she brought his seven-year-old brother back to Tangier as well! From then on the two boys cuddled up together at night and kept each other warm. When they could read and write well enough, they went back home to their village, and their mother was delighted to hear them read God's Word aloud. The boys had loved their time in Patricia St. John's home. In fact, children loved her and God often used that to open their young hearts when she told them about Jesus.

* * *

Smiling at the happy memory of having those two boys in her home, Patricia rose to her feet. It was time for tea with her brother Farnham and his family. Their house was very near the hospital and it had a wonderful view out to the Mediterranean Sea.

'That's just what I need,' she thought, as she walked towards their home. 'A long restful look out to sea.'

'Hello Auntie Patricia!' six children yelled as she went in the door.

Her tiredness disappeared like morning mist as Paul ... and Oliver, Clare, Danny, Martyn and David all rushed to welcome her. How she loved her brother's children!

'Come and see what the grannies are doing,' they yelled, dragging her to the family living room.

'Look!' they said, when they had seen her to a chair. 'They're making cards to send to children in England to tell them about the hospital here in Morocco.'

Patricia smiled and then told them about the missionary books she and Farnham had when they were children, and how Granny St. John had helped make them all those years ago.

'Did you do that too?' Danny asked his Granny Thompson.

'Something of the kind,' the old lady said. 'And your mum loved them as much as you do.'

That night, as Patricia walked back home, she thought about the family.

'I'm fortunate to have lived for so long beside Farnham, Janet and their children,' she decided. 'And to have mother in Tangier too is wonderful. She and Janet's mother enjoy being together. Having both grannies here with us means that we don't have to worry about how they are coping at home. Janet and I look after them between us and the children keep them very happily occupied.'

It was a good arrangement and Granny St. John and Granny Thompson were delighted to live with the family. They didn't even mind the peace and quiet when the older children went off to boarding school.

But Patricia had to admit that there might be a change coming. It had started back in the United Kingdom when she was looking after her mother. A letter arrived from the Rwanda Mission inviting her to write a book about a time of special blessing that had taken place in Rwanda in the 1930s. That time was called the Rwanda Revival.

'It would be so different from mission work here,' Patricia said, when she discussed it with Farnham.

'Very different,' he agreed. 'Here people come to the Lord in ones and twos, where in Rwanda they came in their hundreds in the 1930s. It must have been wonderful to be there then and to see so many people believing in Jesus.'

'Is that what makes me want to write this book?' asked Patricia.

Patricia St. John

Her brother shrugged. 'If the Lord wants you to write it, he'll make you want to do so.'

'It would mean leaving Mother,' she said.

Laughing aloud, Farnham asked if she didn't think that there were enough people in Tangier to look after their mother!

Patricia knew that was true and relaxed as she waited to see how the Lord would lead her.

Early in 1966 she knew what she should do, and Patricia began preparing to move for a time to Rwanda.

'It's quite different from Tangier,' she told her youngest nephew.

'Why?' he asked.

'Let's look at the atlas,' she said, opening it at the right page. 'If you look at Morocco you can see that it's surrounded on nearly two sides by sea. The Atlantic Ocean is to the west of Morocco and the Mediterranean Sea to the north. Do you see any sea near Rwanda?'

David studied the map. 'No,' he said. 'It's surrounded by different countries.' He read their names slowly as they were unfamiliar to him. 'There's Zaire, Uganda, Tanzania and Burundi. The only water I can see is quite far away and it's only a lake.'

'What's it called?' asked Patricia.

'It's called Lake Victoria,' David told her, and then he laughed. 'It's only a lake but it's bigger than the whole of Rwanda!'

* * *

What Patricia St. John noticed when she landed at Entebbe early in 1966 was the clean smell of air newly washed by rain. Then she felt the warmth of her welcome to the home of Joe and Decie Church who had been missionaries in Uganda since 1927.

'Tell me about your early years here,' she asked Joe.

His joyful face melted into sadness.

'They were hard years,' he said. 'Unlike this year when the rains have been good, the rains didn't come then and there was famine in the land. Wild animals, as desperate for food as the people were, even attacked children and ran away with them. The illnesses that spring from poverty spread through the villages and there was fear and sadness and despair.'

'How did the missionaries cope with that?' Patricia enquired.

'They were hit just as the Rwandans were and several of them died, some of their children died too.'

Watching Joe's face as he spoke made his visitor realise just how much he loved the Rwandan people and how he felt their pain and sadness as his own.

'What was the church like then?' asked Patricia.

'It seemed good at first,' he replied. 'But when the going got tough the people were divided. Those who were really Christians continued in their faith. Others, and there were many of them, fell away.'

His eyes lit up as she watched.

'Let me tell you about the day I met Simeoni Nsibainbi,' he said. 'We met at Namirembe Hill and started to talk about what was missing in the church. In the end we went home together and spent hours studying the Bible. And ... there's no other way to put it ... God met with us. He changed us by showing us a little of the amazing beauty of the risen Christ.'

When Patricia left Joe's home to travel to Gahini, where the revival began, she had much to think about. There was also much to see.

'Look at that!' she said. 'These huge hairy cattle are being looked after by such little children!'

Along rough red earth roads they drove, past huts surrounded by fences, and everywhere children appeared to smile their sparkling smiles at the passers by.

'You'll have a treat in just a few miles,' the driver said. 'You're about to see the most beautiful view in Rwanda.'

Minutes later the great mountain ranges came into sight, layer upon layer of mountains with a blue mist settled high on the tops. It took Patricia's breath away. Her heart was still full of the beauty of it when they arrived at Gahini Hospital. As she was shown round, the visitor realised that in all the beauty around her there was deep poverty and need.

* * *

'Where do the women collect water for the hospital?' she asked, seeing them carrying pots on their heads away in the distance.

'They have to go down to the river,' Patricia was told. 'But it's dangerous work as there are many crocodiles there.'

Walking round the wards brought new surprises.

'Who are all these people?' she asked.

'Some of them are patients,' was the answer. 'But most are family members here to look after the people in hospital.'

'Are the three lying together on that bed all patients?' was her next question.

'No, two are family, only the one in the middle is a patient. The two lying under the bed are also members of the family.'

In the midst of all the busyness Patricia discovered that there was love in the hospital at Gahini, and there was healing too.

She was taken to a tiny quiet prayer room, so different from the rest of the hospital, and it was there that Patricia heard more about the revival.

'God brought a young Christian man here; his name was Blasio. For a whole week he stayed in this room and prayed. And it was here that Joe and the hospital matron, who had disagreed about how the hospital was being run, publicly said sorry to each other and to the

Africans who worked with them. Nobody had ever seen a white man apologise to an African before.'

Patricia understood that would make a big impression.

'It was after that that God sent great blessing,' she was told. 'People wept for their sins. Others sang to the Lord for hours and hours and hours – until they had no voices left!'

The visitor listened very carefully to all she was told in order to use it in her book.

'Groups of people went out on missions to the villages. There was such joy, it was as though the villagers were just waiting to hear about the Lord Jesus, waiting to trust in him, and to burst into song!'

'That must have been wonderful,' commented Patricia.

'Yes,' said her guide. 'It was wonderful. But not everyone thought so. For example, the people running the hospital and schools were not best pleased when nurses and teachers left work to go out on mission!'

Thinking what that would be like in Tangier, Patricia could understand the problem.

'Take your time,' Pat Glimer said, as Patricia climbed into a dugout canoe on the shore of Lake Bunyoni. 'We don't want you to fall into the water!'

The water was so still that the lake looked like a mirror. Colourful birds flew around them as Pat paddled towards Bwama Island.

'I'll tell you about the island as we go,' said Pat. 'Bwama Island has a terrible history. It was once the home of a witchdoctor who did awful things. After that it became a colony for people suffering from leprosy. Now we treat them in their own villages, but still some of the older patients, especially those who are badly disfigured, choose to remain on the island.'

'Who looks after them?' Patricia asked.

Pat explained that two English nurses cared for the people who lived there.

'Away back in 1936, some of those who had been blessed in the revival went to Bwama Island to tell the leprosy patients there about the Lord. Two people became Christians and they went into the church to praise the Lord. Then more came, and more, and more and yet more until the church was filled with singing.'

That visit to Bwana Island was very special for Patricia. She saw many people terribly disfigured by leprosy, but working hard and cheerfully.

As she travelled around Rwanda, Patricia listened to stories about the revival, most of them filling her heart with joy. There were others, tales of problems in the church, which made her feel sad. But to write a book about the revival she had to listen to both sides, the good and the bad.

'God's timing was perfect,' Joe told her before she left the country. 'He built his people up in order to help them in the horrors of the war that was about to hit the country. The Lord knew they would need all the help he could give them to see them through those terrible years.'

When Patricia's time in Rwanda was over she went back to Morocco. There she settled down once again with her student nurses, and started to gather her thoughts about all she had seen and heard. Many late nights and much hard work later she finished her book about the Rwandan 1930s revival.

In Search of Onesimus

Hazel St. John packed one last bag in the back of her Volkswagen car.

'Not another thing can go in,' she announced, using her bottom to help her close the door.

'I hope there's room for me,' laughed Patricia.

'I've left you six inches on the front seat,' her sister joked. 'Now get into the car or we'll never get away. I'm sure St Paul didn't carry as much as this with him!'

Patricia laughed. 'I'm quite sure he didn't!'

'How long have you been in Beirut now?' Patricia asked, as the car juddered into life.

'Well, I came out straight after university and stayed for six years,' replied Hazel. 'Then I was home working at Clarendon School from 1944 to 1948 and I've been here ever since.'

'This is 1966,' said her sister, as she did some mental arithmetic. 'So you've been here twenty-four years.'

'If you say so,' laughed Hazel. 'French and Latin were my subjects, not mathematics!'

Patricia could hardly believe this journey was taking place. As Hazel drove carefully out of the city of Beirut, her sister thought back over the events that had brought it about. Long ago, when still a child at school, she had loved the Bible book of Philemon. It's a letter written by St Paul to his friend Philemon about Onesimus, a slave who had escaped from Philemon's household. Paul wrote to Philemon asking him to take his slave back and to see him as a Christian brother because he trusted in the Lord Jesus.

'What are you thinking about?' asked Hazel, as the traffic began to thin and she could think more clearly.

'I was just thinking about Onesimus,' was the reply.

'His story was going to be your very first book, wasn't it? You must have been about ten then.'

Patricia laughed at the memory of her telling her father that she wanted to write a book about Onesimus. He had taken her straight to the library and asked the librarian to show her books that would help her to find out what she needed to know!

'You've written so many books that it would be a pity not to write the first one that you wanted to write,' Hazel smiled at the thought.

'I couldn't write it before now,' remarked Patricia, 'because I can only write about places I've been to.'

'Which is exactly why I suggested we had this holiday following the journeys St Paul made in the Holy Land, Turkey, Greece and Rome. That should give you more than enough material for your book on Onesimus.'

Patricia agreed and felt for the notebook she always carried in her pocket. Noticing people, like Patricia, often carry notebooks to write down memories of what they've seen and heard.

'I have a surprise for you,' Hazel said, as they drove towards Jerusalem. 'I'll tell you about it later.'

'You always were a tease,' her sister laughed. 'I'll look forward to it whatever it is.'

'Close your eyes,' she was told.

About two minutes passed before she was allowed to open them again. By then the whole of modern Jerusalem was laid out before them.

'Wow!' Patricia gasped. 'It's amazing! What a surprise indeed.'

Hazel didn't tell her that her big surprise was still to come.

The following day was spent visiting places that they knew from the Bible, places where the Lord Jesus had walked, told stories and done miracles, and the place where it is thought that he died.

'Now we're going to climb the Mount of Olives,' Patricia was told. 'The view from the top is magnificent.'

It was.

'For the next three nights we're staying with the Keeper of the Garden of the Resurrection, the garden in which it's thought the Lord was buried and arose from the dead.'

Staying in the Keeper's house? Patricia could hardly take it in! Hazel had prepared many surprises for her younger sister, but that was the best one of all.

The Keeper was a Palestinian Arab called Mr Mottar and he and his wife had nine children. During a war between the Jews and the Arabs, not long before the sisters visited Jerusalem, the Mottars had a really hard time. Mr Mottar told them about it.

'We came on holiday to Jerusalem, and when the war broke out we were stuck here and couldn't get back. Every day I went to the bank to see if my family in Palestine had managed to put money into my account. But the days passed and no money came. My children were crying with hunger. I told my family to come and listen to what the Bible said and I read about God giving his people all they needed. "We'll see if God's promise is true," I told them. "I will go out with an empty basket and tell nobody that you are hungry. If I come home with my basket empty, we'll know that the Bible isn't true. If I come home with food in my basket, we'll know that the Bible is true."'

Hazel and her sister listened spellbound to the story.

Mr Mottar took a sip of tea. 'I went to the bank but there was no money there for me. Then I met a friend. He asked how I was managing to live with all the children in these hard times. Because I'd said I'd tell nobody how poor we were, I smiled and said we were fine. My friend went away and my heart felt hollow. I was so sad I just sat down by the side of the road and prayed that the Lord would give us what we needed. When I opened my eyes,' said Mr Mottar, 'my friend was standing in front of me. "You can't possibly be all right with so many children," he said, and put a packet of money in my basket. There was enough money to feed us for several days! And then I was given the job of Keeper of the Garden of the Resurrection and we've had enough to eat ever since. God is so good!'

Patricia agreed with Mr Mottar, God is good – very good.

Having spent some time in the Holy Land seeing places Jesus saw, and walking where he had walked, the sisters headed off to follow the footsteps of St Paul ... first stop Antioch.

'It's really nice of your friends to have us to stay in Antioch,' Patricia said. 'Tell me about them.'

'They're a very rich family,' commented Hazel, 'and the daughters are pupils in my school.'

Hazel was Headmistress of the Lebanon Evangelical School and Training College in Beirut.

'I think we should stop and tidy ourselves up before we go to their home,' she said. 'Let's find a river where we can bathe. We're both so dusty we look as if we've just spring cleaned a cow shed! And I'd like to wash the car too, if possible,' she added. 'It would look awful sitting outside their house in the state it's in!'

Just then a very grand car drove along the road towards them.

'I'm going on to the verge to let it past,' said Hazel. 'It looks like the President's car coming.'

Patricia peered at the on-coming car to catch a glimpse of the President. The car slowed down and then drew to a stop beside them. There was no president inside, just the family they were going to stay with coming to meet them … dusty sisters, dirty car, and all! The family turned their car and drove in front of Hazel to show her the way. So, in a little procession of two, one very grand car drove into Antioch followed by a tiny, filthy car full up of camping gear and two very dusty middle-aged women!

'I'm so looking forward to going to Homaz,' Patricia said, a day or two later. 'Homaz used to be called Collossae, and that's where I'm going to set the story of Onesimus because it was from there that he ran away.'

They drove higher and higher into the hills to reach Homaz.

'No wonder Onesimus wasn't caught after he escaped,' thought Patricia, looking at the rough countryside through which they were travelling. 'You could easily hide here without being seen.'

'I think we'll go right up the track and into the market place,' Hazel said.

She had been before and had worked out where

best to go. Suddenly they were surrounded by a crowd of people who didn't often see tourists. At that time people didn't go on holiday to Turkey as often as they do today. Using sign language the people tried to speak to the two sisters. Hazel and Patricia were given such a welcome! After a while someone in the crowd remembered a man in the village who spoke English. A group rushed off to find him. When the poor man arrived his reputation bit the dust. The only English he knew was, 'See you fellows in de morning'!

Everywhere they went Patricia took notes to help her write Onesimus's story. She also drew little sketches of the places she visited, just to remind her of the shape of the hills and where the rivers ran. But one place they visited needed no notes taken because she knew there was no chance whatever of forgetting it.

'It was wonderful to spend a night with the children in the Bible camp,' Hazel said, as they drove away from Thessalonica. 'They were so full of joy as they sang to the Lord that their young faces shone.'

Patricia laughed. 'And our faces were red with embarrassment this morning, weren't they?'

'Well, we thought we'd found a nice quiet beach where we could have a swim,' said Hazel. 'Or we wouldn't have stripped off our dresses and gone into the water.'

'It was a pity that a group of local Christians had decided to hold a prayer meeting just around the headland. We were much more embarrassed than they were,' Patricia laughed. 'In fact, they didn't seem in the least bothered.'

'If they hold regular prayer meetings on the beach they might be quite used to such goings on!'

Day after day there were new and interesting things to see. The sisters often had their Bibles out and open at the Book of Acts in order to see what had happened in the places they visited. They finished following in the footsteps of St Paul after three days spent exploring the ancient parts of Rome.

'This can go away now,' said Patricia, putting her Onesimus notebook into her bag. 'Now I'm really on holiday!'

Already the book *Twice Freed* was being written in her mind. But first there was a trip to Florence, Spoleto, Assisi and Monte Carlo as well as the many other interesting places they visited before driving all the way back to the ferry over the mouth of the Mediterranean Sea to Tangier.

Just a few miles from their ferry port, their car was rammed from behind by a huge truck. Thankfully neither Hazel nor Patricia were hurt, though their car certainly was. There was a fiesta in the town and the sisters couldn't find a single hotel that could take them. Eventually someone led them through dim and dingy lanes to the door of a little house. It was really quite a scary experience as neither Hazel nor Patricia spoke much Spanish. The door opened and an old woman took them into her home. Suddenly they realised by the Bible texts on the wall that the Lord had led them to a Christian home. There were over sixty thousand people in the city, only about sixty of them Protestant Christians, and their hostess was one of them! Although they had to leave Hazel's badly damaged car in Tarragona to be repaired, and they had to arrange to complete their journey to the ferry by train, they did so with happy hearts having spent the night with one of God's chosen people.

'Everything's gone so well on our holiday until now,' Hazel commented to her sister the next morning.

'True,' agreed Patricia, 'but no doubt God has a reason for the mishap with our trusty old Volkswagen.'

It was just a short time later that they found out what that reason was. All of a sudden they met an English lady standing weeping on the pavement.

'Can we help you?' Hazel asked, in English.

The woman looked up in amazement.

'Did you speak English to me?'

Hazel smiled. 'Yes,' she said. 'We're both English. Can we help you?'

'Oh please help,' the stranger said desperately. 'I don't know what to do.'

'Let's sit down on this bench and you can tell us

119

your story,' Patricia suggested.

'My sister brought me out here on holiday. I wasn't really enjoying it,' the woman admitted. 'I don't like crowds and I was frightened by not being able to speak to people because I don't know any Spanish. My sister did all the talking. But then she took a stroke and she's seriously ill in hospital. I just don't know what to do and my sister's too ill to help me.'

Having shared her problem, she burst into floods of tears.

The look that passed between Hazel and Patricia said, 'This is why God allowed us to have that accident. He knew this poor woman needed our help.'

Within an amazingly short time Hazel and Patricia, who had travelled so much that they knew how to cope with emergencies, had made all the arrangements. By the time they left their new friend, plans had been made for her sister to be taken to the airport by ambulance and for them both to be flown home to England.

Leaving Tangier

'What are your grannies for?' asked a little boy who was visiting Farnham's children.

David St. John looked puzzled. He didn't understand the question.

'The grannies in my village make bean mash and bring water from the well,' he continued. 'But your grannies don't do either.'

Grinning, David thought of the long list of things that his grannies did.

'They help look after us,' he began. 'They listen to everybody's problems. And they teach the nurses English to help them if they go abroad to study.'

His young friend was very unimpressed. David decided to bring out the big guns.

'And my Granny Thompson once sewed on a man's head that was half cut off!'

That had the reaction David hoped for.

'She what?' his friend gasped.

David repeated what he had said in a totally ordinary voice as though his Granny Thompson sewed on heads every morning before breakfast!

'How did that happen?' asked the seriously impressed village boy.

'Granny and Grandad Thompson were missionaries in China. Granny Thompson was a doctor there and one day she had to treat a man whose head was half cut off. She sewed it back on again and the man got better.'

Granny Thompson was very surprised a few days later when the same young boy came to visit.

'Will you tell me how to sew on heads, please?' he asked her politely.

Granny suggested that he should start by learning how to bandage fingers and only move to sewing on heads if he qualified as a doctor.

By the late 1960s both grannies were becoming older and frailer and more and more of Patricia's time was taken up in helping care for them.

'Would you like me to read to you?' she asked most afternoons.

The old ladies loved Christian books, especially those that told the lives of people who trusted in Jesus. Patricia settled down in between them so that they would both be able to hear her and then started to read. She knew exactly what would happen. After a few pages one would begin to nod off to sleep, and a few pages later the other would join her. Patricia would read until their breathing told her they were comfortably enjoying their nap and then she would change to a book she was reading herself. When the grannies wakened up again half-an-hour later, she would continue reading the book she had been reading to them!

* * *

Having been happily settled in their routine for some time, the years that followed brought so many changes into the St. Johns' family life that it was difficult to keep up with them. Janet, Farnham's wife, went back to England to be with the children through their boarding school years.

'I'm sure that she's right to do that,' Farnham said to his sister when they talked about it.

Thinking back to their childhood, when their father was abroad and all the St. John children were in England, Patricia agreed with him.

Farnham looked thoughtful. 'Now I know how hard it was for Dad to stay in South America without us. This house feels so empty and yet so full of memories of happy times.'

A year later, in 1975, Patricia was concerned about her older brother.

'Farnham's very ill,' she decided, as she mopped his forehead with a damp cloth to try to bring down his temperature. 'I'll get a doctor from the hospital to come and look at him right away.'

'You were quite right to bring me over,' the doctor said, having examined his patient. 'Farnham has typhoid fever. He's going to need careful nursing to see him through this.'

Day after day Patricia provided the careful nursing her brother needed. Farnham slid in and out of consciousness as his sister prayed by the side of his bed. She thought of Paul and Oliver, Clare and Danny, Martyn and David back home in England, so far away from their daddy. She thought of Janet, a splendid doctor, who knew how ill her husband was as a telegram had been sent to tell her. 'Janet must be wishing she was here to help,' thought Patricia. 'But she's helping by her prayers, and the children will be praying too.'

Day followed day and Farnham seemed to be getting no better until one morning, when Patricia was caring for him, his eyes opened and he looked as if he was taking in what was happening.

'Praise the Lord!' whispered his sister. 'He's past the worst.'

Having been a nurse for so many years, she knew that Farnham was on the mend.

While he was recovering but still seriously ill, news came from the Moroccan government. Patricia wondered how to tell her brother the news without doing damage to his fragile health.

'I'm afraid that there's bad news from the government,' she began. 'It seems that they want us out of here. They're claiming the whole hospital compound, including your own house and Dar Scott.'

Farnham, ill though he was, knew the right questions to ask.

'What about the Moroccan people who work here?'

'The government will employ them in the hospital.'

'And those from overseas?'

'They can apply for jobs here too,' his sister told him.

'Will they buy our houses from us?' he asked.

'No,' she said. 'They're taking them without paying for them.'

'How long have they given us to get out of Morocco?'

'We've to leave within three months,' Patricia replied. 'It's not long.'

'Have you told the grannies?' was Farnham's last question.

His sister nodded. 'Yes,' she assured him. 'I've told them. But they didn't really take it in.'

'They're not fit to move,' he said.

Patricia smiled. 'I'll stay here in Tangier with them. The government won't mind that as I won't take anything to do with the hospital. We can find a little flat and I'll care for them there.'

Struggling to his feet, Farnham walked shakily to the Outpatients' Department which was filled with local people who were upset when they heard the news.

'What will we do without Dr St. John?' someone asked.

'There he is!' another shouted.

'Are you going to leave us?' people asked from every side.

Farnham, almost too ill to stand, tried to reassure people that the hospital would stay open. They would still have health care. More and more people crowded into the Outpatients' Department as news spread that Farnham and his sister were there. Eventually so many people gathered that lives were in danger and the police had to be called out to send them home!

As soon as it could be arranged, Janet flew to Tangier to help with their final packing. She was so relieved to see her husband was getting better, but concerned that he shouldn't exhaust himself with all that had to be done before they left.

'I think we've found somewhere for you to live with the grannies,' Farnham said, a short while later. 'It's a flat over a grocer's shop in the native quarter of the town. Unfortunately it's a difficult stair, but after the grannies are up they won't need to come down again.'

Janet smiled. 'God has chosen the time for this,' she said. 'The grannies don't really know what's happening and they're quite happy spending their days lying side by side in their twin beds being cared for. After the move I don't think they'll even notice that they're not where they used to be.'

'I don't think they'll even notice we've gone,' said her husband rather sadly. 'And I should be grateful for that.'

* * *

'Tomorrow is our last day here,' Farnham thought, as he took his final walk round the hospital.

At each bed he paused and prayed for the patient lying in it, and for all the patients he remembered who had lain there over the years. Face after face passed through his memory. Some were faces of those who had become Christians and who now lived for Jesus in their villages, hard though that was for them. Others were faces of people who had made life really hard for Christians, especially their fellow Moroccans.

'I treated them all the same,' thought Farnham. 'In fact, I probably tried to be even more loving to those who were most difficult to like.'

The following day, when Janet and Farnham left for the airport to fly out of Tangier, the streets were crowded with local people sorry to see them go, some of them weeping quite openly at the loss of the doctors they loved.

'Its really good to have you here,' Patricia told Hazel, not long afterwards. 'It's so strange without Farnham and Janet.'

'I'm sure it is,' her sister agreed. 'And I'm only sorry that I can just spend two weeks with you before I have to go back to Lebanon. But let's try to make the most of it. You really need to relax when you can as it's hard work looking after the grannies.'

'Zohra is a great help,' assured Patricia. 'She's almost

like a member of the family.'

'Let's ask her to do all that needs done tomorrow and we'll go down to the sea,' Hazel suggested. 'The grannies won't even know we've gone.' Then, very quietly, she added, 'I don't actually think Mum recognises me.'

'Nor me,' admitted Patricia. 'But both grannies recognise love and so long as they're being loved they're happy.'

A restful day at the beach gave the two sisters strength for what was to come. Just a few hours after they arrived home their mother died peacefully as they sat, one on either side of her, holding her hands. When Janet was out visiting her mother not many weeks later, Granny Thompson died. Once again Patricia had family with her when the Lord knew she needed help. While both Patricia and Janet were sad, there was joy at the thought that their loved ones were home in heaven with Jesus.

Two or three weeks later Patricia, who was still in Tangier, heard news that really shook her.

'I'm sorry to have to tell you that Clarendon School has burned down,' she was told over the phone from England.

'Clarendon School?' Patricia said. 'Clarendon School burnt down?'

The words didn't seem to make sense to her. She thought of buildings she had grown to know and love while she was home looking after her father and mother in North Wales. It wasn't the school as she knew it in Malvern, but the new Clarendon. It had burnt down!

Meaning began to sink into Patricia's brain. No lives were lost, and how grateful she was for that. 'But my aunt?' she thought, quite stunned by what she was struggling to understand. 'She's not hurt because she was away overnight when it happened. But she's lost everything!'

Patricia sat down and tried to think. 'Poor Aunt,' she said aloud. 'My poor dear aunt!'

A day or two later she heard that her aunt had moved to live with her brother John and his wife in Coventry, in the midlands of England. He was a doctor there, although he was in poor health himself.

'I think the time has come for me to go home,' Patricia thought, as she looked out of the window of the Tangier flat. The grocer's shop beneath her window was busy with afternoon trade. People wove through the street below and she watched them and listened to them. It was as though the sounds were coming from very far away, as though she wasn't part of what she was seeing around her.

'Yes,' said Patricia quietly but firmly. 'The time has come for me to go home.'

Home ... and Away

It was 1976 and Patricia St. John was beginning to settle down in Coventry. She made her home with her brother John and his wife, Gwynne, and their family. Some of the children were old enough to have left home, the younger ones were still there, and it was a treat for them to have Aunt Patricia come to stay. All of her life Patricia had been popular with children and teenagers, and John's family just loved her.

'What can I do to help?' Patricia asked her brother and sister-in-law. 'I'm here. I'm fit and I'm willing to do whatever I can.'

'I could certainly use you in the surgery,' John admitted.

His sister nodded, she knew from looking at her brother that he was far from well. He had an illness that made him shake so that even writing was difficult.

'I'll do whatever you need,' she assured him. 'I believe that's what I'm here for.'

'I know Aunt would really appreciate if you could spend time with her,' Gwynne commented. 'She's having to build up a life here from absolutely nothing. All that survived the fire was what she had with her in her overnight bag.'

A wave of sadness overtook Patricia at the thought of her aunt, who had spent her life serving other people, suddenly having nothing.

'It'll be a privilege to do what I can for her after all she's done for me,' said Patricia. 'It will be a way of trying to thank her.'

So it was that life for the Coventry branch of the St. John family settled down to some kind of normality. Patricia was there to do the increasing number of things with which John needed help, to be a strength and support to Gwynne, and to spend time with her nephews and nieces. She was also there to do all she could for her much-loved aunt. There were a lot of people in Coventry who needed her. Then, in 1978, something happened that changed things.

'Hello,' a voice said over the telephone. 'I'm Hazel's friend.'

'Is she all right?' asked Patricia.

'I'm afraid she's had an accident,' the long-distance caller said. 'But she'll be all right.'

'What's happened?'

'Oh, Hazel had a fall and fractured her femur. But she's had surgery and is all pinned together again. They'll let her out of hospital in a few days, as soon as she can walk with crutches.'

'Do you think I should come out to look after her?' offered Patricia.

'Not yet,' Hazel's friend assured her. 'She'll speak to you herself when she comes home.'

The next phone call brought more bad news.

'I'm home now,' said Hazel, when she and her sister had said their hellos.

'And is everything all right?' Patricia asked.

There was a pause from the other end of the line.

'Is everything all right?' Patricia repeated, thinking she hadn't been heard.

'I'm not bad,' Hazel said, 'but the flat above me took a direct hit the other night and there's water seeping down here. There's been more fighting than usual. Maybe it's as well that I was in hospital as there are even bullet holes in some of my books.'

'I'll come out as soon as I can,' said Patricia firmly, only to be reminded by the voice at the other end that she was Hazel's little sister.

'You'll do no such thing,' was the reply. 'I'll be fine.'

However, older sisters don't always get their own way. Hazel needed help. It was bad enough that she was on crutches - it certainly didn't help that there was a lot of fighting in Beirut.

Having landed at Beirut Airport, Patricia climbed into a taxi and gave the address.

'That will be £30,' said the taxi driver, holding out his hand for money before he even started the engine.

'Why is it so much?' his passenger asked. Thirty pounds was a great deal of money.

The driver didn't have much English, but he was able to explain why the fare was so high. He mimed shooting a gun and said, 'Pop! pop! pop!' as he did so.

Patricia understood. There was still fighting in the city and it was a long detour to get where she wanted to go. She decided to find a braver taxi driver who would go a more direct route and not cost so much!

Despite her protests, Hazel was pleased to see her sister, and Patricia did all she could to help her.

'I have plenty of help in the house,' said Hazel. 'What I most need you for is to drive me around the city when I want to go out.'

Patricia's eyes opened wide. 'You want me to do what?' she said.

'You heard me,' Hazel told her, and just for a minute her sister could hear the headmistress speaking!

'You'll be fine,' insisted Hazel, on their first outing in the car. 'Just do what I tell you, and do it quickly!'

All went well at the first few corners but then Patricia was suddenly surrounded by cars and all the drivers were hooting their horns at her.

'Who has right of way here?' she asked desperately.

'Whoever gets in first!' Hazel said. 'So put your foot down!'

A few corners further on the same thing happened again. Patricia had to shout over the noise of car horns.

'Go right!' Hazel told her.

'We can't! It's a one-way street!'

'Just go right,' her sister insisted. 'The other road's blocked and this is the only way out of the snarl-up.'

Patricia swung the car round and drove the wrong way up a one-way street. She was quite sure that policemen were lurking in every doorway, but not a single person seemed to notice! When she eventually parked the car and helped her sister out Patricia was exhausted!

For five weeks she stayed in Beirut and helped Hazel as much as she could. She even felt less guilty driving the wrong way along streets by the time she had been there for a month.

'I'll be home next week,' Patricia told John on the phone.

'Will Hazel cope without you?' he asked.

Patricia looked at her sister. 'She'll manage perfectly well. If you could see her now you'd discover that she can get round like an animated kangaroo on her crutches. And she uses them to switch on the light, push up the window, pull books along the floor to where she's sitting, reach things down from high shelves, not to mention tapping me awake should I nod off from sheer exhaustion after driving her half-way across the city.'

135

John laughed. 'Then it's probably time for you to come home,' he admitted. 'Otherwise you may need looked after yourself!'

Patricia's five weeks spent in Beirut among bombs and bullets were tucked away in her memory for future use. She was still a noticing person and she knew that life there would make a good background for a book. In the two years that followed her time in Beirut she wrote **Nothing Else Matters**, which is based on the true story of a family she met there.

In 1980, when Farnham was just sixty-two years old, he died. Patricia was heartbroken. She knew Farnham was in heaven with the Lord Jesus Christ, but she felt as if a bit of her had died too.

'I can't bear to think what it must be like for Janet and the children,' she wrote to a friend. 'I miss him till my heart aches and it must be so much worse for them.'

During the three years that followed a great weight of sadness hung over Patricia. It was like carrying a heavy bundle where her heart used to be and she felt as if it would never, ever go away. Strangely it was another death that led to her burden being lifted. John died in August 1983 and Patricia, who didn't feel able to go to church the following Sunday, went for a walk in the local wood. As she meandered through the dappled light, it was as though she heard a voice speaking to her, the voice of her Father God. 'I will not leave you comfortless,' the voice said. 'I will come to you.' And with those gentle words her heavenly Father began to remove the burden of sadness from his weary daughter.

By then Patricia had her own little home. What she didn't have when she moved in was very much money. And setting up home is an expensive thing to do.

'I know the family would help me if I asked them,' she thought. But the only one she told was her Heavenly Father.

'I wonder who this is from,' said Patricia, as she picked up her mail one morning.

The postmark told her that it had been posted in the Lake District. Slitting the envelope open, she took out an official-looking letter and read it.

'It's from a lawyer asking me if I can prove my identity,' she said in a very puzzled tone. 'He says he's been looking for me for a year.'

Of course, Patricia could easily prove her identity. Her passport was one of her most well used possessions. Another letter followed a few days later.

'It gives me pleasure to inform you that you have been left the sum of £1,800, to which has been added £200 interest over the last year. You will find a cheque for £2,000 enclosed.'

The letter went on to say that the money had been left to her in the will of an old lady she had never met. The lady had read one of Patricia's books and it had helped her. She left the money by way of saying thank-you. And never was a cheque for £2,000 so much needed by Patricia St. John as that one was. When she counted up all that she was due to pay it came to £1,700.

'I'm so glad that it took the lawyer a year to find me,' she told the Lord in prayer. 'For it is today that I need the money; I didn't need it a year ago.'

Patricia St. John was not alone in her new little home for she took her aunt to live with her and they settled down happily to life together. Children and young people had always gathered round her, and they continued to do so.

'What are you building?' a teenager asked, as he passed the house one day and found Patricia taking mugs of coffee out to some workmen.

'It's a garage,' she said. 'But it's not going to be used for a car.'

'So what is it going to be used for?' puzzled the boy.

'That's where I'm going to put the snooker table,' she told him.

'The snooker table!' he laughed. 'You must be joking!'

But Patricia wasn't joking. She did whatever she could to encourage young people to come to her home in order that she could befriend them and tell them about the Lord Jesus.

'Can I see the snooker table?' the same teenager asked some weeks later, having heard from his friends about a tournament Patricia was organising for the young people in the area.

'Of course,' she said. 'Come in and have a game. There are some others already there.'

Auntie was interested in all that was going on, even though she was very old. But her special interest, not in England but far away in Africa, was the Emperor of Ethiopia's grandchildren, five girls whom she had loved from the day they arrived at Clarendon School. When a revolution broke out in Ethiopia they and their mother, along with other women in the royal household, were captured and put in prison. For years she prayed for them, wrote to them, and arranged for things they needed to be sent out to their prison.

But Patricia's aunt's life came to an end in 1984 when she died and was taken home to heaven. Although she was sad to be without her aunt, it gave Patricia real pleasure to think of the one she loved being able to hear the voice of Jesus after being totally deaf for most of her long life.

A New Beginning

'I've never seen anything like it,' Hazel said, as she and her sister watched the television news. 'How can reporters get into Ethiopia to film starving children when nobody can get to them with food?'

Patricia could hardly see the screen through the tears that were streaming down her face.

In 1984 there was a terrible famine in the Horn of Africa, and the worst hit country of all was Ethiopia. For the very first time television cameramen brought back newsreels of starving children with swollen stomachs and arms and legs like sticks. Cameras zoomed into their poor faces, where flies crawled all around their eyes. Mothers were shown sitting holding their dying children and looking as if they were dying themselves. People all over the world were shocked by what they saw. Such television news pictures are common today and we have become so used to them that they no longer shock us as they should do.

'Can you help us to do something for the children in Ethiopia?' a neighbouring child asked Patricia and her sister a day or two later. 'The people there are starving.'

'Bring your friends round and we'll talk about it,' suggested Hazel. 'We must do something.'

Within a very short time plans were made for a Christmas sale and the children were all very busy working out what they could do.

'I usually buy a bag of crisps each day, but I'm saving that money to send to Ethiopia,' a nine-year-old boy said. 'And my big brother says they're going to have sponsored games of snooker in your garage to raise more money.'

Patricia smiled. Some people thought she was unwise to have teenagers in and out of her house, but they respected her and she trusted them. She wasn't at all surprised that they wanted to raise money for starving children in Ethiopia.

'Mum says I can sell the toys I've outgrown,' a girl told Patricia. 'And she's going to make new clothes for the dolls so that they'll sell for more money.'

'The children and teenagers have worked so hard,' Hazel said, on the morning of the sale. 'I hope they are pleased with the money they raise.'

The sale itself was a very noisy, happy affair, with children trying to count up what people had to pay, and their parents and friends being quite happy to pay more than the marked prices. After all, everyone saw the television news each evening and reports from Ethiopia were not getting any better. When the sale was over and everything packed away, Patricia's sitting room was filled with exhausted and excited boys and girls all wanting to count the money.

'That will buy a lot of food!' one of them said, when the counting was over. 'And I'm going to watch the news to see our food being delivered.'

'Would you be prepared to go out to Ethiopia?' Patricia was asked at the beginning of 1985. 'You're very involved in the work of Global Care and it would be good to have someone out there to let us know how best we can help.'

It took her hardly any time to agree to go, although the thought of seeing such awful sights was not pleasant.

'You're leaving England at a lovely time of year,' Hazel commented, a few days before her sister left. 'There are still some primroses in bloom, the bluebells are out, and now the pink campion is opening up. Let's go for a walk in the country before you leave.'

There was a shower of rain just before they went for their walk, and the raindrops glistened in the sun making the wild flowers look even more beautiful than usual.

Four days later Patricia was in a Land Rover on her way to a refugee camp in Ethiopia. It was 120 degrees. There wasn't a single blade of green grass to be seen. Everything was dust coloured because everything was covered by dust. Carcasses of animals lay drying in the glare of the sun, and in two or three places in the far distance there looked to be glimmers of water, but there was no water there. The sun was just playing its mirage tricks on hopeful and desperate eyes.

'Tell me what's happening here,' Patricia asked her driver.

'The people arrive at the main camp,' the man answered. 'There are about 80,000 people there. Our camp is an overflow, and we get about 1,400 new people coming each day. They are brought in by lorry, though a few walk here themselves.'

The following morning she saw it all for herself.

'You go and help them off the lorries,' Patricia was told, and she arrived at the lorry stop just as the first one drove in.

'Hello,' she smiled, as she had no words in the local language.

Taking their bony hands she helped the children off first. No adults made a move before all the young people were off.

'How can they look so happy?' she wondered, as starving children smiled at her. Then she realised that they were just so glad to have arrived, so glad to still be alive.

A boy of about fourteen had no strength to climb down from the lorry.

'Let me help you,' she said, putting her arms round his stick-like body.

Bracing herself against his weight, she almost fell backwards because he weighed so little. Patricia laid him on the ground very gently in case she should hurt him. When all the children were off, those who were too ill to help themselves were lifted to the ground. Only then did the others climb down.

'It's so quiet,' thought Patricia. 'These poor people have done all their crying weeks and months ago. They have no tears left now and no energy to speak.'

For most of the month she was there Patricia worked in the babies' feeding centre, where tiny scraps of babies were fed by tube or had drops of milk dripped into their mouths from a spoon.

'They need to be wrapped up warmly,' she told a new helper. 'Their little bodies are cold because they've not enough food in them to keep themselves warm, even in this hot climate.'

'Where did these blankets come from?' the helper asked, as she wrapped a skinny baby in a blanket made of knitted coloured squares.

Patricia smiled. 'I don't know where that one came from, but I do know that there are women, even very old women, back home in the UK who knit blanket squares. In fact, I know a lady who never watches the television news unless she's knitting a blanket square. She says that there's so much bad news in the world that she has to do something to help, and that's the only thing she can do.'

'It must be good for the children to see these lovely coloured squares,' the other woman said. 'All they've ever seen in their short lives is the colour of dust.'

'I must remember to tell that knitting lady what a difference these blankets make,' thought Patricia. 'She'll be so pleased.'

'Are you writing again?' Hazel asked her sister, after she'd been home for a few months.

Patricia laughed. 'Of course I am. I'm always writing!'

'I take it this book is based in Ethiopia,' suggested Hazel.

'And you'd be quite right. I think I'll call it *I Needed a Neighbour*.'

'The children here will be really pleased to read it. It will help them to understand what it's like out there.'

Patricia looked up from her typewriter. 'Things are beginning to get better in Ethiopia now,' she said. 'But it'll take years and years for the country to be anything like normal again.'

'Aunt would have been so glad to know that the five girls she prayed for have been set free, along with their mother and the other women,' Hazel said. 'I think she prayed for them every single day.'

'For a very long time,' agreed Patricia. 'They were in prison for fourteen years altogether.'

* * *

After her visit to Ethiopia Patricia St. John became more and more involved in Global Care. The work of the charity grew and it was able to help in more and more countries.

'You're not working on another book, are you?' Hazel demanded one day.

'No, I'm not. I'm counting my blessings.'

'What do you mean?' asked her sister.

Patricia grinned. 'I'm making a list of all the countries in which Global Care has been able to help, because I want to thank God for them.'

'That's a good idea,' was the reply. 'And I'm sure the young people who have done so much fund-raising for Global Care would be delighted to help you count your blessings because they'd be counting their blessings too. They've been able to help so many people, but working together has also helped them.'

Patricia nodded in agreement.

'Do you want to hear my list of blessings?' she asked.

Her sister certainly did.

'We've been able to send money to projects in Ethiopia, of course, Morocco, Uganda, Sudan, Bangladesh, India, Lebanon, Mozambique, Zimbabwe, Turkey and now in 1991, we're sending money to Romania too, where there are so many poor children abandoned in state orphanages.'

Hazel sat back in her chair and smiled.

'I'm glad you made that list of blessings because it's so much easier to think about the world's problems than to remember the good that is being done.'

Patricia agreed and then reminded Hazel of Global Care's motto. 'You can't change the whole world but you can make a world of difference to some children in need.'

Patricia St. John lived for a further two busy years. Had she kept a diary over that time, it might have read something like this.

'Busy in and around the church all day. Had young people to the house after the evening service. Discussed how to raise funds for relief work in Rwanda. They are full of bright ideas and they have so much energy too. It's great when they use their energy to help others.'

'School holiday today so we had eight or nine children visiting us for the morning. They wanted to know all about the work in the mountain village in Morocco. Then they discovered about Hazel's school in Lebanon so asked if they could come back in the afternoon to hear more about it!'

'Spent most of the day writing letters. I get quite a number of letters, especially from children who've read my books. All of them get a reply, and some of them write back again immediately! Quiet evening for a change.'

'Our boys' and girls' arts and crafts class that started in our home is now so big that it meets in the church hall. We do some really quite adventurous things together. And, as the children keep coming, we think they must enjoy it. Of course, we always have a Bible story and prayer at the end.'

'We had a little boy visiting us today. I hid some small Easter eggs in the woods before he came, and he had such fun looking for them. After finding his fourth egg, he looked up at Hazel and said, "Do you think the Patricia bird will lay another egg?" How I love children! Perhaps I've never really grown up myself!'

'The teenaged boys are in the middle of a snooker tournament out in the garage. They know to come for prayers before they go home. One of them came in to tell us that they'd be later than usual this evening and we'd not to go to bed until they'd finished so that they could have a Bible reading and prayer time together.'

'We had a busy house today and that's not unusual. It's so good to have a home with an open door. People who live round about sometimes come in just to talk, but we often have friends from overseas too. Although this is just a small house, it seems to have elastic walls!'

'A lady from down the street came today. She and her family have real problems. At first I thought she was going to ask for money, but what she really wanted was someone to pray with *her. Hazel and I both prayed. We've told her she can come back any time she needs to talk.'*

In the middle of all her usual busyness, and after a very short illness, Patricia St. John died in her sleep on 6th November 1993. The children and young people who lived near her were especially sad to lose their friend. Hazel, who missed her sister very much indeed, kept reminding them, and reminding herself, that Patricia was in heaven with Jesus, whom she had loved and served since she was young herself.

Patricia St. John
Life Summary

Patricia St. John was almost born on an ship during a storm in the Bay of Biscay. Her parents were returning to the United Kingdom from South America where her father had been teaching in a Bible school. However, soon after the ship docked at Southampton, a near nasty accident started Mrs St John's labour and the little girl was born, four weeks early but safe.

Patricia's childhood was mainly spent in Malvern with her brothers and sister in the beautiful countryside there. Those days of fun and freedom inspired her first book for children, *The Tanglewoods' Secret*.

One evening, when Patricia was six years old, she realised that God loved and cared for her. It was his love that motivated and empowered her to serve others throughout her life.

When Patricia was seven, and Mr St. John was still working as a missionary overseas, his family moved to Switzerland for a year. This later inspired her second book, *Treasures of the Snow*.

Nursing in London during the war was very stressful and tiring. She experienced the dark side of life, which contrasted with her blissful childhood. Her poem *To what purpose?* expresses those tensions.

Soon after the war her brother, Farnham, went to

Morocco to work as a surgeon in a missionary hospital.

Patricia decided to join him and in her autobiography she describes the journey riding on the back of her brother's motorbike.

Morocco also inspired Patricia in her writing as her next book Star of Light draws closely on her experiences in the northern mountains of Morocco. For four years she cared for the poor people among whom she lived, using her house as a dispensary and visiting many surrounding villages as well. Eventually she was asked to leave the area because the officials disapproved of her sharing her Christian faith. Patricia returned to Tangier and set up a nurses' training school attached to the hospital.

The hospital was taken over by the government in 1974 but Patricia stayed on to nurse her mother and Farnham's mother-in-law. She returned to England after her mother's death, eventually living with her sister, Hazel, in Coventry. Many of the local children and young people were captivated by her stories and sense of fun. She wrote *The Mystery of Pheasant Cottage* based on this time of her life.

Patricia's books were translated into so many languages that hundreds of thousands have read them and been helped to believe in Jesus as their friend and Saviour.

This text is edited and adjusted from the web page:
www.patriciastjohn.org.uk

Thinking Further Topics

Chapter 1: Fun and Games

The young visitor in the story thought that everyone knew about Jesus. Was she right to think that? Do you think everyone in your town or street knows about Jesus? Many people today, even in busy modern cities, have not heard about the Lord Jesus Christ. Some think they know about him because they have heard the Christmas story, but they need to know more than that. What do they need to know?

Chapter 2: Goodbye and Bonjour!

One day Patricia was listening to a story about a girl who copied the following verse from the Bible: 'I have redeemed you; I have called you by name; you are mine' (Isaiah 43: 1). When Patricia heard that story she knew that she wanted to belong to Jesus too. You belong to your family, but do you belong to Jesus? Think about him. Why would it be good to belong to Jesus Christ?

Chapter 3: Growing Years

God knows everything about our lives, even the things that we keep secret from everyone else. Patricia realised that she wasn't really living a Christian life because she hardly ever read her Bible or prayed. Do you love to read God's Word? Do you long to speak to God in prayer? Or are these things pushed to the side because you'd rather watch T.V. or read a magazine?

Chapter 4: Nurse St. John

Patricia didn't get to study medicine as she had hoped to do, and the young man that she had hoped to marry was killed during the War. These things were difficult for her, but she believed that Jesus could help her and he did. What problems do you have? Are you worried? Do you feel discouraged? Jesus can help you too.

Chapter 5: Tangier!

As a missionary Patricia sometimes had to travel to distant villages to teach people about God. At other times she just invited people over for a cup of mint tea. God's Word spoke to many people through what Patricia said. Zorah heard that Jesus wanted to give her rest and she had never heard that before. In what way did Jesus give Zorah rest?

Chapter 6: Mountain Villages

When Patricia and Fatima wanted to be invited to speak at a particular village what did they do? What amazing thing did God do then? It is good to realise that sometimes when annoying things happen, and things don't exactly go to our plans, God has something else in mind. His plans are always the best.

Chapter 7: Sad Goodbye

When Fatima was taken to the prison what secret message did she manage to pass on to Patricia and how? Think about your life. If the police were after you because you'd become a Christian, how would you get the strength to keep going? The Christian life is not easy, but God can give you strength.

Chapter 8: No Veils!

Patricia helped a young Moroccan Christian to understand about forgiveness. What do you feel like doing when someone is nasty to you? It can make us feel sad and mad. But we must obey God's Word. God tells us to love our enemies and do good to those who are mean to us. Can you think of times in your life when it was really difficult to show forgiveness? Can you think of times when someone forgave you?

Chapter 9: Dad

Patricia's father had worked as a missionary in Brazil, a long way away from his family. Sometimes God asks us to do difficult things and make hard decisions. But when we trust in the Lord with all our hearts and acknowledge him in all our ways he will guide us. Acknowledging God means telling others that we trust in Jesus and showing them that we really by obeying his Word. Do you use your lips and your life to tell your friends about how great Jesus is?

Chatper 10: Choose One

In Rwanda during the 1930s there was a revival: a time of great blessing from God when a great many people asked him to forgive them. One man described the time of revival as God meeting with them. The people were changed by seeing a little of the beauty of Christ. In what ways can Jesus be described as beautiful? Do you understand what true beauty is? It is not your skin or your looks.

Chapter 11: In Search of Onesimus

Mr Mottar was in a desperate situation and God helped him. When the Lord gave him the money to feed his family he knew that God was true and that he cared. Think about what God gives you every day. What gifts does he give you to show you that he cares for you? What does he give you to show you that he is true?

Chapter 12: Leaving Tangier

After Patricia had been in Morocco for some time God had other plans for her. He had planned all of her life. He had planned that she became a nurse rather than a doctor and God used her as a nurse in Morocco. God had planned that she work in a boarding school and tell children stories, and he had used those stories too. Think about the things that you learn and enjoy. How might God use these things to spread the gospel in the years to come?

Chapter 13: Home ... and Away

Patricia had bills to pay. Just when she needed it, a cheque arrived. The money had been left to her a year before, but why was Patricia glad to receive it just when she did? The Bible tells us that before we ask God for something he will answer. So if God already knows what you need, why do you need to pray? God wants you to spend time with him. Praying to God is good for us; it changes us. That is why God wants us to pray. That is why we need to pray.

Chapter 14: A New Beginning

Even as an elderly lady Patricia led a busy life, a life of busyness for God. If you think that you can't do much for God, remember that, 'You can't change the whole world but you can make a world of difference to some children in need.' Remember this too, it is God who changes peoples hearts. But he can use you to reach out to just one person so that he or she can hear of Jesus, perhaps for the very first time.

OTHER PATRICIA ST. JOHN BOOKS AVAILABLE FROM CHRISTIAN FOCUS PUBLICATIONS:

For children:

The Safe Place

Prayer is an Adventure

A Young Person's Guide

A Home for Virginia

Twice Freed

For adults:

Life Everlasting (Previously published as A Missionary Muses On The Creed)

Patricia St. John
Timeline

1918	Women given the vote in the U.K.
1919	Patricia St. John born.
	The first transatlantic flight completed.
	The pop-up toaster is invented.
	The Treaty of Versailles is signed ending the First World War.
1926	The first public demonstration of television in the United Kingdom.
1928	The first film with spoken dialogue is shown in the U.K.
1929	Wall Street Crash.
1931	Mohandas Gandhi agrees to suspend civil disobedience in India.
1938	First refugee children in the 'Kindertransport' arrive in U.K.
1939	Britain declares war on Germany.
1940	Winston Churchill becomes Prime Minister.
1942	First American troops arrive in U.K.
1943	Patricia St. John starts work at St Thomas's Hospital, London.
1947	Patricia enters a writer's competition and *Tanglewood's Secret* is published.
1949	Patricia St. John goes to Tangier, Morocco.
1950	*Treasures of the Snow* published.
1952	Elizabeth II becomes Queen.
1953	The structure of DNA is discovered.
	Star of Light published.

1956	Patricia St. John returns to the U.K.
1965	Patricia St. John goes to Morocco.
1966	Patricia St. John visits Rwanda.
	Patricia and Hazel St. John journey in the footsteps of St Paul.
1969	Concorde: the world's first supersonic airliner makes it's first flight.
1970	*Twice Freed* published.
1975	The Moroccan government orders the St. Johns out of the country.
1976	Patricia St. John returns to the U.K.
1978	Patricia St. John visits Beirut to care for her sister.
1979	Margaret Thatcher becomes Britain's first female Prime Minister.
1980	Farnham St. John dies.
1982	*Nothing Else Matters* published.
1984	Famine hits the Horn of Africa.
1985	Patricia St. John visits Ethiopia.
1987	*I Needed a Neighbour* published.
1989	The World Wide Web is invented.
1991	Operation Desert Storm and the Liberation of Kuwait begins.
1992	Channel Tunnel opens linking London and Paris by rail.
1993	Patricia writes her autobiography.
	Patricia St. John dies.
2004	*Prayer is an Adventure*, republished.
2007	*Life Everlasting*, republished.